Just Ask Us

Just Ask Us

A Conversation with First Nations Teenage Moms

Sylvia Olsen

WINLAW, BRITISH COLUMBIA

Library and Archives Canada Cataloguing in Publication

Olsen, Sylvia, 1955-
    Just ask us : a conversation with First Nations teenage moms / Sylvia Olsen.

Includes bibliographical references.
ISBN 1-55039-152-6

    1. Indian women—British Columbia—Social conditions. 2. Indian girls—British
Columbia—Social conditions. 3. Teenage mothers—British Columbia—Social conditions.
4. Indian women—British Columbia—Health and hygiene. 5. Indian girls—British
Columbia—Health and hygiene. 6. Teenage mothers—British Columbia—Health and
hygiene. 7. Indian youth—British Columbia—Social conditions. 8. Indian youth—British
Columbia—Health and hygiene. 9. Coast Salish Indians—Social conditions. 10. Coast
Salish Indians—Health and hygiene. 11. Teenage pregnancy—British Columbia. I. Title.

E99.S21O34 2005   305.2352'089'9794   C2005-906617-2

Sono Nis Press most gratefully acknowledges the support for our publishing program
provided by the Government of Canada through the Book Publishing Industry Development Program (BPIDP), the Canada Council for the Arts, and the British Columbia Arts
Council.

All royalties from *Just Ask Us* directly support Tsartlip First Nation's youth programs.

Edited by Katherine Gordon, Dawn Loewen and Margaret Tessman.
Cover art by Caleb Beyers
Photographs by Tom Kerr
Design and digital imaging by Jim Brennan

Published by   Distributed in the U.S. by
Sono Nis Press   Orca Book Publishers
Box 160   Box 468
Winlaw, BC V0G 2J0   Custer, WA 98240-0468
1-800-370-5228   1-800-210-5277

books@sononis.com
www.sononis.com

Printed and bound in Canada by Houghton Boston Printers.

To the young moms who generously shared their lives with us
and who enthusiastically wanted this book to be written

and

to all teen moms and dads who courageously take on
the task of raising their children.

Acknowledgements

Thank you to the Aboriginal Healing Foundation and Tsartlip First Nation for supporting the research project.

Thank you to Lola James for working with me throughout the study; to Peggy James, Marion Tom, and Judy Stein for advising us; and to everyone who generously supplied us with information.

Enormous thanks to the young moms and dads who took part in the study and whom I cannot name, for enriching my life and for the lessons they taught me.

Special thanks to the young moms who edited countless versions of this conversation and advised me many times of numerous necessary changes. Without you this book would have been rudderless.

I appreciate Tom Kerr's patience with me as I endlessly talked about my feelings, ideas, fears, cautions, and excitement about this project.

Special thanks to Heather and Yetsa for, once again, allowing me to share their personal story.

It has never been more true that the mistakes are mine and the improvements are theirs. Thanks to the people who helped me with this book: editors Katherine Gordon, Dawn Loewen, and Margaret Tessman; idea editors Janet Dunnett, Ron Martin, Diane Harris, Julia Bell, Chris Nichol, and Heather Goulet; publisher Diane Morriss; designer Jim Brennan; art contributor Caleb Beyers; and models Fawn Jack and family.

Prologue

On Monday, March 24, 1997, my fourteen-year-old daughter, Heather, came into my bedroom before school and tearfully announced that she was pregnant. On Tuesday, March 25, 1997, she gave birth to her daughter, Yetsa.

I had no idea I was about to become a grandmother, unless I count a dream I had had the previous November. It was one of those dreams that was too real to ignore, so I asked Heather, "Are you pregnant?" She looked astonished and said, "No, of course not." I needed to believe her more than I needed the truth so I was satisfied. And anyway, why would Heather be pregnant? Within the context of our life pregnancy made no sense at all. Heather was a good girl. She danced, did her school work, hung out with her girlfriends, and gave me no reason to worry about her.

At first, everyone on both sides of Heather's family was shocked by the news of the baby. After the initial surprise, however, my family's reaction became very unlike that of her father's family. Culture and social location determined how our families would respond to her having a baby at such a young age.

Ours is a cross-cultural family; three of my children are part Coast Salish and the fourth, a late addition, is a black Portuguese Brazilian who had come to live with us five years earlier when he was thirteen. We live in a First Nation on Vancouver Island, British Columbia. Our social life is divided like the road we live on, with the reserve and First Nations culture, the children's father's world, on one side of the street and white middle-class Canada, where I come from, on the other side. The children are all biracial and see themselves as walking down the middle of the road when it comes to colour and culture.

Teenage pregnancy and parenthood, like many other social issues, are treated very differently in the two sides of their world. Almost immediately, after the shock had worn off Heather's First Nations relatives, they crowded around the new baby, welcoming her into the family. My family didn't counter with such open arms. It took some time, some rejection, and a great deal of eye rolling before Heather's white relations fit her new situation into the family scene. They had no comfortable, ready-made place for what had just happened.

After Heather gave birth, teenagers with babies became a topic for discussion with almost everyone I met. While the First Nations side of our family openly received Yetsa, they remained shocked that *Heather* would become pregnant. Somehow, because of her half-white status, they thought she should be immune from the trend of very young women in First Nations having babies. On the other hand, many of our non-Aboriginal friends and relatives accounted for Heather's pregnancy in the context of her First Nations status. "It's common for First Nations girls to get pregnant, isn't it? First Nations people just accept teenagers with babies, don't they?" But no matter where people were from or to what culture or religion they belonged, the same questions arose: "What are you going to do about it?" "What is Heather going to do?" "What is the best thing to do now she has a baby and is still only fourteen?"

I had been acting head of our family since my husband left a few years earlier and alone when it came to child-rearing decisions. I have to admit my response to Heather and Yetsa was based more on instinct than anything. I had no time to weigh the pros and cons of how to approach the situation, so along with Heather and the other children we came up with what made sense to us: Heather and Yetsa would be fully incorporated into our family. Heather would be Yetsa's primary caregiver. Everyone would help Heather with the baby, and, I wasn't sure how, at some point Heather and Yetsa would form their own family, independent of the rest of us, and move out on their own.

It has been eight years and I can say that's just about how it happened. The story between these two bookends is filled with many more decisions—some good, some not so good—and a whole lot of trial and error.

But this book isn't my family's story. It's about a group of First Nations teenage women who became pregnant and who, like Heather, had to face motherhood at a very young age. It's about the decisions they have made, their own trial and error. In this book are the answers they gave to questions such as *How did this happen? Why did it happen to you? How do you cope?*

Just ask us, said these young women, and we will tell you.

Introduction: Our Conversation

It is the girl's auntie who persuades her to take part in the mother's group for teenagers. Her auntie says, "I sure could have used something like that when I had your cousin. I didn't know a thing, didn't have anyone to talk to. I thought I was the only girl in the world who was stuck at home looking after a baby." Her auntie phones her over and over again and tries to talk her into attending, but the girl doesn't want to go at first. Play group on Wednesday mornings is okay; her son likes playing with the other kids. But the girl hides in the corner while the nurses and experts and other moms talk. They barely acknowledge she is there and that is fine with her.

At first the girl thinks that being part of a talking circle or a focus group will direct too much attention her way. She will have to talk and she doesn't feel like talking. She will have to be careful that she doesn't say too much and she doesn't feel like being careful. She doesn't want people to know what is going on in her life or how she feels about it. Her life is miserable, she is a lousy mom, and her son will forgive her someday. That's all that matters.

At the first focus group the girl listens mostly. She keeps her mouth shut and watches the group leaders and other girls talking. They talk about everything. Everyone seems to be interested in what everyone else is saying. The girl tries to keep her mouth shut until the session is over but she can't. She lets a few things out about her son's temper tantrums. Then later she says she wishes guys didn't like sex so much. She feels kind of weird saying those words right out loud like that but then the other girls jump all over it in agreement. "Right. You aren't kidding."

During the second and third group meetings the girl talks a lot more. Sometimes she doesn't want to stop talking. The other girls laugh when she tells her stories. The week she is upset, two of the girls cry when she cries. They say they understand exactly how she feels and she believes them. At first the girl worries that after the sessions the other girls will all run out and tell everyone what she said. Now when she looks around as the words leave her mouth she feels that it doesn't matter. Her stories aren't scary anymore. They don't need to be secret. The girl realizes her words are like her face and her ponytail; they are part of her and she is proud of what she says. She begins to feel that her ideas and her feelings belong to her—her inside and outside are the same body. She begins to feel as if she knows herself and that she no longer has to pull a lid over what might come out of her mouth.

Now the girl thinks about the presentation. The group leader asked her and another young mom to talk to a group of teenagers from the local high school. They are going to speak to a group of girls and a separate group of boys. The girl is shocked that she said yes. She is shocked that after she thought about it she didn't back down. And she is even more shocked that she is actually looking forward to talking to the group.

The girl doesn't know which words she will use. She knows she wants to ask the teenagers some questions and she wants to tell the boys that sex for girls isn't great all the time. But she isn't sure whether once she gets there she will say those words exactly.

When the time comes, the room is full of boys and the girl can feel the palms of her hands are greasy. Her stomach feels as though if she ate anything it would come right back up. Her brain is a jumble of words. Not one word is in any kind of order that anyone would understand.

The girl sees the facilitator nod her head when she finishes the introductions. She hears her name and then the room is quiet. For a fleeting second she wonders whether the boys want to hear what she has to say. The next second she feels like some other girl—one she has never met. Then the girl feels like a girl who knows who she is; she can feel her feet on the ground and her head on her shoulders. She begins by telling the boys that she realizes having a baby isn't just hard on the young mom; she says it must be awful hard on the dad as well. In the middle of her presentation she asks the boys what they would do if their girlfriend wanted to have an abortion. At the end the girl finishes with a tearful, sobbing explanation of what she had dreamed of before she got pregnant and then she excuses herself for crying and tells the boys how much she loves her baby boy.

As the girl speaks she watches the boys' faces. She knows them all; she shared classes with them in high school. Usually they can't sit still. But they never move while she speaks. They listen to every word she says. When she finishes, the boys say, "Wow" and "Heavy duty, man" and then they ask her questions like "How do you pay for stuff?" and "Who looks after you when you're looking after your kid?" and "How do you ever get to school and get your homework done?"

The girl answers their questions and when she is finished

they thank her. They say she must be brave to be able to stand up there and talk like that. Brave isn't something she has ever thought about herself. Total chickenshit is the closest to brave she has ever been. But she has to admit when she hears her own words she sounds strong. When she listens to her own story it sounds bold. After she speaks and after the boys listen she realizes she is more than she has ever thought. She realizes she has never lined her life up in a story like that. No one has ever really listened like that. When the girl walks out of the workshop, she is stronger than when she came in.

Up to 70 percent of new First Nations families on southern Vancouver Island, British Columbia, are starting with teenage mothers and, in many cases, teenage fathers as well. These young parents alone cannot do much to improve the conditions of their lives. If society helps them manage for the few years while their children are young, they are more likely to succeed in finishing their education, finding jobs, and becoming responsible adults. Their children will be less likely to become teenage parents themselves, and will have every chance of leading independent and productive lives.

Breaking the cycle of teenage parenthood requires an understanding of history, social conditions, and cultural influences. It also requires society to pay attention, not simply to pass judgment. Teenage parents cannot do it alone, nor should they have to try. And the problem, while most serious in First Nations communities, is one that many people in Canada should be discussing.

Just Ask Us is intended to become part of that discussion. It is a labour of love and a record of the strength and courage of young women who face enormous challenges, often with few resources. At its heart are the voices of thirteen young First Nations women who participated in our focus groups. I am writing this book as a grandmother and community member, who along with many others wants to better understand young women and improve their life circumstances when they become young mothers. I am also writing for the young mothers so their concerns and attitudes have a voice. Another reason I'm writing this book is that front-line workers, social workers, and others who work with youth asked me to include them in the conversation—they wanted to know what the young moms had to say.

I hope *Just Ask Us* will stimulate ideas, in part, simply by presenting the voices of young First Nations women and giving their perspectives on their own experiences. But, of course, the conversation is not just for or about First Nations people. For too long, Aboriginal Canadians have been excluded from mainstream Canadian society, as if their concerns are not the same as everyone else's in this country. But all Canadians share the same problems, if to varying degrees and for different reasons, and our struggles to contend with our problems are relevant to each other. What affects First Nations affects Canada, and what affects Canada affects First Nations.

I have lived on an Indian reserve for more than thirty years. I am not Aboriginal, but my ex-husband is Coast Salish, as are my children. When my teenage daughter had a baby I spent the next five years talking about teen pregnancy and parenting in First Nations communities. But I began to realize that, like most people in the community, I was only talking. I wasn't doing anything. So when a health worker from a neighbouring First Nations community suggested that I develop a research project on the subject and work with some young parents, I readily agreed.

The project was designed in 2003 with other mothers and grandmothers in local First Nations communities and funded by the Aboriginal Healing Foundation, a national organization addressing the legacy of residential schools. Certain elements of the project were fundamental: the research was to result in action, and was to be presented with respect for the young women interviewed and their communities, as well as for Aboriginal people in general.

Knowing the tension that exists between scientific research and the kind of community-based study that we had designed, we weighed the pros and cons of facilitating the study ourselves as "insiders," or hiring an outside researcher. But while independent researchers would bring credibility and impartiality to the study, and while the participants might reveal things to a stranger that they wouldn't to someone they knew, we decided to do things a different way.

Driving the project was a strong desire for a community discussion, in much the way that people talk to their neighbours and their families, and the only way to achieve that was to let the community lead and have insiders facilitate the research. First Nations people have been researched by professional "outsiders" for generations, and have been left with little sense of positive results in their communities. Trust in independent research conducted by non-Aboriginal people is therefore very limited. The community certainly wanted the information. But it also wanted a relationship between the participants and facilitators that would have lasting benefits. Therefore I led the project together with a local First Nations woman who has experience working with young people.

In addition, we did not feel compelled to bring independent literary, sociological, or scientific analysis and background to the research project. In any event, at that time there appeared to be no comprehensive studies or discussions of on-reserve teen parents. We simply wanted to hear the stories of First Nations teen parents based on their own experiences, in order to learn directly from those most affected. We wanted to start at the very beginning of the conversation.

The process for conducting the research was community driven and organic in its development. We had wanted, for instance, to include young fathers in the project. Unfortunately, while we received more than enough expressions of interest from young women, we initially had no response at all from young men.

The thirteen young mothers who did participate were between fifteen and twenty-four years old. We created two groups: in one, seven teenage mothers; and in the other, six mothers twenty to twenty-four years of age who had birthed their children while they were teenagers. We interviewed the participants both individually and in groups. The interviews were not necessarily formal. Sometimes together, sometimes separately, the groups went out for dinner and had picnics, baby showers, and birthday parties, building relationships and trust and creating a strong camaraderie among the participants and facilitators.

After a few months several young men who had heard good things about the project decided to take part. But because the young women had so much more to say than the young men, the voices heard in this conversation, unless otherwise stated, are those of the young mothers.

We examined existing local community programs designed for young First Nations parents; interviewed community front-line workers, elders, and grandparents; and surveyed local health, nutrition, and birth control services. Our advisory group—a nurse, an elder who was a residential school survivor, and a grandmother who had been a teenage mother—kept us on track, sharing their personal experiences and perspectives on the best way to work with the young women.

We asked the young women questions about family, school, community, friends, boyfriends, relationships, finances, self-image, sexual habits, use of birth control, abortion, pornography, health services, sexual abuse, birthing, parenting, discipline, dreams, education, future plans, love, fear, and more. They shared coping strategies—how to deal with being out in public, how to make forty dollars last a week. They told us about their personal needs and fears and some deeply hidden aspects of teenage mothering.

We also realized there were things they didn't want to talk about. Sexual abuse and violence were two subjects acknowledged but generally avoided. Some spoke about how sexual abuse and violence has affected their lives, and wanted to know how to protect their children, but they did not want to talk about their own abusive or violent experiences. We had decided from the outset that our role as facilitators was to listen to what *they* wanted to talk about—we were not investigators or counsellors—so we did not push into the areas that seemed to be off limits.

There are significant limitations on recording a conversation such as the one set out in *Just Ask Us*. First Nations communities are small, and the only way to keep details of the participants' lives confidential was to obscure particular features of their quotations and stories. Their privacy was too important to risk the use of pseudonyms or any other potentially identifiable characteristics. In order to record the conversation with the greatest authenticity possible under those circumstances, I have therefore used a number of different voices. My voice as a community-based researcher is both narrative and analytical. The sidebar quotations come mainly from the young women, and the stories that open each chapter are fictionalized but based on actual stories we heard.

This is not an academic treatise or a textbook. The events and experiences recorded here are real. The statistics speak for themselves; so have the young women involved.

As community researchers, we found the data gathered both surprising and fascinating. As a storyteller, I felt driven to write this book. One reader of an early draft was disinclined to believe some of the stories in it. I assure you they are true. They are challenging, sometimes appalling, and always compelling. But within them lies hope: that by telling these stories, and opening up the conversation, the future will be different.

1

Wʜᴀᴛ's ᴛʜᴇ ᴘʀᴏʙʟᴇᴍ?

The girl listens to her history teacher talking about First Nations. He says they helped the Europeans adapt to the Canadian climate and environment. If it weren't for the Indians the newcomers wouldn't have survived. But then the story changes and the teacher says that First Nations peoples were pretty much annihilated, at least that's how it sounds to the girl. First, disease, alcohol, and displacement, and then the reserves and residential schools, and then to make matters worse the teacher starts talking about statistics. Holy, the girl thinks, does he know how that makes us feel? She squirms in her seat. Blah, blah, blah. The girl doesn't listen to the numbers but to her it sounds as though if you are a First Nations person you are 1,000 percent more likely to have everything awful happen to you, from AIDS to suicide to house fires. Shut up with that stuff, she thinks. She squirms some more. She looks around the class and sees her cousin Ernie. His arms surround his head, which is plunked on his desk. Then she looks at the part Mohawk guy who sits at the back of the room. He has a snarly look on his face. The girl can tell he is as uncomfortable as she is.

Maybe this stuff is right, she thinks, but does the history teacher need to put it out there like that? Doesn't he know that there are real people here and now, like me and Ernie, that he's talking about? And all those statistics—doesn't he know how they make a kid feel? It's like if you're First Nations you don't have a chance: something's gonna get you.

The girl wants to put her hand up and say something to change the subject, but she doesn't want to call attention to herself. She just wants him to shut up.

Finally the teacher quits and then it is worse—the kids start asking questions. She follows Ernie's example and hides her face in her arms and pretends to fall asleep.

Teenage motherhood is not new, and it is not confined to any particular culture or society. For as long as anyone can remember, families, communities, churches, and governments around the world have been dealing with the moral issues and difficult life circumstances associated with young people having children. In fact, most families have a story of a young woman with a baby. If you go back even two generations, you are likely to find a grandmother, mother, aunt, sister, or cousin who had a baby while she was a teenager.

In many European families, the young woman's name may have been forgotten, the baby's name grafted discreetly onto another family tree. Young unmarried mothers were often sent away from home to live with relatives, or to a boarding home or church-run institution. Sometimes they left the baby with strangers and returned home hiding a few extra pounds as if nothing had happened. Some stayed away to make new lives for themselves, and their names have been permanently erased from their family's memory and records. The dates of birth and ages of some young women and their babies who do appear in family histories have often been painstakingly adjusted to fit the cultural and social expectations of the time.

Until recent decades, for the most part, stories of unmarried teenagers with babies were kept hidden in family closets—places where no one ever went, or wanted to go. In the last few decades changes to adoption information policies and shifts in public attitude have resulted in the reunion of countless families with those lost generations of young women and babies. All the same, attitudes surrounding teenage sexuality, pregnancy, and parenthood remain inconsistent and contradictory.

North American culture insistently and enthusiastically sells sex, which at the same time it claims it doesn't want children to buy. The inherent contradiction is evident at both ends of the spectrum of views on the subject.

One approach to teenage sexuality champions abstinence, limits access to birth control and sex education in schools, and seeks to ban safe and available abortions. Yet some of the same people who promote that approach are also profiting from the vicarious sale of sex to young people through alcohol, cars, music, fashion, health products, nightclubs, and almost everything teenagers see, hear, touch, and smell.

At the other end of the spectrum is open support of teenagers' rights to freedom of sexual experience, access to sexually explicit material, and freedom to have abortions. Yet no one knows the future for a society that supports such teenage freedoms, but which either cannot afford or does not wish to pay for the social programs that may be needed to cope with the results.

In First Nations communities, the story is the same in many respects. In other respects, it is completely different. In fact, there are so many young Aboriginal women with babies that each one is hardly a story at all. Front-line community health workers now estimate that nearly 70 percent of First Nations families on southern Vancouver Island reserves are started by teen parents such as the ones involved in our project. Most of the new mothers and fathers appear to be between the ages of fifteen and seventeen. While couples in Canada's broader society are beginning their families later and later in life, First Nations families are getting started younger and younger.

Social statistics reveal in stark terms that First Nations families in British Columbia (and almost certainly throughout the rest of Canada) are in crisis. From 30 to 40 percent of status Indian babies born each year are mothered by women less than nineteen years of age. From 1991 to 1999, 25 percent of teenage mothers in the province of British Columbia were status Indians, while status Indians accounted for somewhere between 3 and 5 percent of British Columbia's total population. During the same period, the status Indian live birth rate for teenage mothers was 193 per 1,000 live births—four and a half times the rate for all other residents of the province. For Aboriginal women under fifteen years of age, the rate of births is estimated to be as much as eighteen times that of other Canadian teens the same age. The figures are disturbing, especially at a time when the number of teenage mothers is decreasing in Canadian society as a whole.

Although First Nations communities share many of the concerns and sentiments of all Canadians regarding teenage sexuality, pregnancy, and parenting, neither a total abstinence approach nor a total freedom approach adequately describes how First Nations communities look at the issues. An entirely different set of cultural perspectives and circumstances are brought to the subject instead.

In the past, First Nations communities had traditions that involved taking care of young women when they became pregnant. Life was sacred; therefore women, the bearers of life, and babies, the gift of life from the Creator, were held in high regard. Once a woman gave birth, she enjoyed an elevated status in her community. When a baby was born it was honoured, incorporated into the extended family of the community, and raised as part of that community.

However, First Nations communities have for some time been experiencing incompatibility between traditional ideas and modern practices. Many of the old ways have been disrupted or discontinued, and the ones that are left are not effectively controlling the number of teenage pregnancies. Nor are communities taking care of the young mothers and their babies in the manner of the past. Although most First Nations people know of the problems involved, having a baby and sometimes two babies before a young woman turns twenty has become a normal rhythm of life, and little if anything seems to be happening to change it.

Young parents are often unable to take on the full responsibility of parenting their children, and are unprepared to support themselves financially. This causes a ripple effect: an unrelenting strain on the economy and social well-being of First Nations communities, which simply do not have the resources to support the growing number of teenage parents and their children. First Nations community workers generally agree that what is needed is the promotion of responsible and safe sex, support for teenage parents, education on parenting skills for young parents, help to enter the job market, and opportunities for their children. But modern, busy, and often chaotic families cannot fill the gap left by the dissolution of traditional family practices, and First Nations children are now being fostered out to non-Aboriginal families in record numbers. Nothing seems to be stopping the flow.

Of course, certain elements are common to the families of teen parents in all societies and cultures. For example, they are more likely to be poor than families started by more mature adults. Teen parents are not responsible for their poverty—teen births are a consequence of being poor. Women living in poverty have more babies and have them younger than women from more affluent social groups. More First Nations people live in poverty than any other group in the country, and First Nations communities have more teen parents than other groups in Canada. But poverty alone does not account for this story. History, community conditions, and culture all are relevant to understanding the issues.

In the work of First Nations professionals such as Cindy Blackstock, a member of the Gitksan nation who works in the field of child and family services, and Kim Anderson, a Cree/Metis writer and educator, we find described a complicated set of circumstances resulting from colonial events and practices that were imposed on First Nations and that for some time have been having a dire effect on First Nations families.

From the late eighteenth century to early twentieth century, bouts of smallpox, influenza, and tuberculosis took a massive toll on Aboriginal children and old people, decimating populations. Another devastating blow was enforced acculturation during the first sixty years of the twentieth century. Church and government officials took more than 20 percent of First Nations children from their families and culture to stay in residential schools, where they were acculturated in the ways of European religion and society. Many of these children were also physically or sexually abused at the residential schools. When the schools closed—many of them as late as the 1960s—a diaspora to non-Aboriginal foster homes began. Entire sets of siblings were removed from their homes by social workers and fostered or adopted out to non-Aboriginal families, often a long way away.

Simply put, since the first European explorers came to Canada, traditional family systems and children not only have been put at risk, but have become outright casualties. For more than a century, First Nations communities in British Columbia suffered a tragic breakdown in their social order. The result has been that their young people are now experiencing a higher incidence of alcohol and drug addiction, sexual abuse, violence, sexually transmitted infections, suicides, and vehicle accidents than any other group of young people in Canada.

Today more First Nations children live apart from their families than ever. There are three times as many First Nations children in care today than were in residential schools at the height of their operations in the 1940s. First Nations children make up more than 50 percent of all children in care in British Columbia, and between

30 and 40 percent of children in care nationally. Between 1995 and 2001, there was a 71.5 percent increase in the number of status Indian children from reserves being placed in child welfare. The trend continues.

At first glance, poverty, social disruption, and lack of opportunity could be seen as primary causes of the high number of teen parents in First Nations communities. Drugs, alcohol, and sexual abuse, combined with a low level of education and job readiness, create an environment conducive to unplanned pregnancy. The reasons seem simple enough—that is, until the idea that First Nations societies have been devastated is considered fully and that, as Kim Anderson believes, "The political, social, emotional, and practical response to [this devastation] has been to reproduce *in spite of it all*" [emphasis added]. She argues, "It's simple: when a people are under siege it is imperative to reproduce." First Nations have suffered great losses over the past century and the greatest loss was that of their children. Therefore, Anderson states, both conscious and unconscious efforts have been made to reproduce. It's working: First Nations are the fastest-growing segment of Canada's population. Some estimates indicate that more than 50 percent of the First Nations population in Canada consists of ages twenty-six and under.

Also relevant to the discussion is the cultural context. As noted, in the traditional world view of Coast Salish First Nations, all children are a gift from the Creator. Children are therefore to be loved, cared for, valued, and respected, no matter what their circumstances might be. A couple that had many children was considered blessed. Even today it is natural that a child is accepted into the family without hesitation, regardless of the age of its mother.

Keeping the baby is without question. Choosing to put a baby up for adoption outside of the community is almost unheard of among First Nations. Traditional beliefs strongly oppose abortion. The spirit of a conceived being has a life of its own and the mother and father do not have a right to end the physical life of that spirit

25

My family is really family oriented. Although they live all over the place they are really starting to see themselves as a family and every new baby is important. My family has lost a lot of kids to the system. Some of my family didn't make it home from residential school, they have been adopted out, we've had suicides, you name it. Now they want to make sure every baby becomes part of the family no matter who the baby is born to. My cousin had a fetal alcohol baby and the little boy had all sorts of health problems. He was in foster care but the family brought him home. So when I got pregnant the family just got excited that it would have another baby.

under any circumstances.

Of all the contributing factors, poverty remains the most compelling. In Canada the story of the "haves" and the "have-nots" is nowhere better illustrated than in the contrast in standard of living between Aboriginal and non-Aboriginal communities. Economically, First Nations are the poorest communities in this country. Most reserves have been fully financially dependent on the federal government for more than a century. Many first-time visitors to an Indian reserve in Canada remark how much it looks like a community in a Third World country—sometimes despite the fact that the reserve is surrounded by million-dollar private homes in a wealthy non-Aboriginal city or rural area. Statistics tell us that three out of five Aboriginal children under age six live in poverty, and that 73 percent of Aboriginal single mothers are poor compared to 45 percent of non-Aboriginal single mothers.

Times are changing. First Nations people are building independent economies, reforming health and education delivery, reviving culture, and improving governance as ways to raise the standard of living in their communities. However, the challenges are enormous, and much frustration arises from the fact that change takes time. It is already taking too much time for young people today who are caught in the middle.

Why should non-Aboriginal Canadians care about any of this? Two reasons stand out. First, Aboriginal children are the future of their societies, yet they are highly at risk and marginalized. They are being taken into care in higher numbers than ever before and continue to be the most underprivileged people in Canada. Many of today's children will have children before they are ready because they had teenage parents who lacked skills for parenting and creating a family. The disruption of First Nations families is not a thing of the past: it is continuing today. And since what affects the part affects the whole, it has social and economic ramifications for all of us.

Second, First Nations teen mothers are key to the success of First Nations' goals to build strong communities. They are the women who determine the strength of families and the health of their young people, and who pass on critical cultural information to the next generation. Teen mothers are a vital First Nations resource, and the cost of ignoring them is too high.

2

WHO WE REALLY ARE

The girl collapses the stroller, slings the diaper bag over her shoulder, wraps her baby over her arm, and struggles up the stairs of the bus. He fusses uncomfortably, but then her arm is cutting right into his poor little stomach—hurting him and killing her.

She quickly scans the bus for empty seats. None. At least none that she won't have to share with another passenger. It is one of those days when everyone has a seat to themselves. She will have to double up. She looks cautiously from one passenger to another, hoping to catch a hint that someone won't mind sitting next to a snotty, tired kid, stroller, diaper bag, and exhausted mom.

The bus lumbers down the road and then suddenly jolts to a stop at the traffic lights, sending the girl tumbling into a seat without calculating whether or not it's friendly.

"Do you mind?" she asks, half-smiling apologetically as she crams the stroller against the woman's leg.

The woman half-smiles back through clenched teeth, barely hiding her disgust.

The girl stuffs the diaper bag under the seat, lays the

stroller in the aisle against her foot, and settles her baby on her lap. The woman sucks air through her teeth like a steaming kettle and hunches her shoulder toward her as if she is afraid she might catch something.

Her baby's whine grows into a grumble. The girl checks her pockets for tissue when his nose starts to bubble. Forget tissue; she wipes his nose with the end of her sleeve and smears the dribble across his chin.

Please, baby boy. Just half an hour and we'll be home.

The girl sees, or maybe she feels, passengers' eyes staring when her baby's grumbles turn into a whimpery cough. She wipes his nose again and bounces him on her knee.

Please, baby boy.

Her baby's cheeks flap up and down as the bouncing becomes almost hysterical.

I know you're hot and tired and fed up with shopping and sitting, but we'll be home soon.

The woman shoots her an angry look when her baby's foot bumps the woman's leg.

"Oh," says the girl. "I'm sorry."

She stops bouncing her baby and, as though someone pulled a cork out of his throat, his whimpers burst into a wail. Looks pierce the girl's body from all angles like icicles. And if it isn't bad enough that her baby won't stop screaming, he starts a coughing fit at the same time. It will be at least twenty minutes until they get home. Every empty seat is now filled.

In spite of the racket her baby is making, the girl overhears a woman's voice coming from a seat behind her. "That baby is sick. That young girl shouldn't have him on a bus."

"She doesn't look more than about fifteen years old," replies a man.

"God, those Indians have babies young," says the woman.

Please, please, please, baby boy.

Hot salt burns the girl's eyelids. She wants to bolt from the bus at the next stop, but she is miles from home with no bus transfer and no money.

God, you have a pair of lungs on you, boy. Can't you be quiet?

There is only one way to pacify her baby but the girl can't do it there. Not on the bus. It feels like a prison cell she has been thrown in, guilty of being one of those Indian girls who screw around and have babies. She doesn't have to see the other passengers' faces. She feels their disapproval seep through her pores. She doesn't have to hear their words. The tone of their mumbles is enough for her to know what they think.

The baby blanket is folded into the stroller. She'll never be able to get it. Her sweater is in the diaper bag. There is nothing around to cover up with so the girl yanks up her T-shirt and bra, exposes her breast and stuffs her baby's face onto her nipple. He sputters and snuffles and shouts and coughs one last time and then sucks furiously.

The girl's skin burns as silence falls over the bus. A man turns and glares at the girl's face and then at her breast. Disgustedly he finally unlocks his eyes and looks away. The woman next to the girl angles sharply toward the window when she hears sucking sounds.

"It's about time," says the woman from behind.

"Yeah, but the poor baby," the man says.

The picture in Canada of First Nations young women with babies is a downtrodden image that is decades old, and a stubborn stereotype actively affecting young women today.

Despite the common perception that racism is on the decline

in our country, negative stereotypes persist in the harm they cause. Young First Nations women with babies may not know the history behind the stares they get when they walk down the street, but they do know how bad it feels. Public transit, for example, is not a feel-good place for First Nations teen mothers. The young women in our groups said it felt as though everyone was looking at them, especially when their baby was coughing or crying and they couldn't find a way to keep him quiet. Whether or not anyone really was staring didn't matter, because it always felt as if they were and there was nothing they could do about it.

Talking about negative stereotypes is also difficult. It can be uncomfortable for non-Aboriginal people. For First Nations, it can be far worse than merely uncomfortable. Elders advised me not to perpetuate vicious ideas and words that have been said about their people for generations, and to find ways to tell the story without repeating words that never should have been said in the first place. "The young people," an elder told me, "don't have to hear it all again.

I was training at work and this guy keeps coming up to me and talking. Finally he says to me, "You're not like other Indian girls." I'm, like, what am I supposed to say to that? Thank you? So I say, "What do you mean?" "You know," he says, "I mean there's a stereotype Indian girl and you aren't like her." He didn't want to say what that was. I say, "So you are saying I'm not a chug. Well, thanks." How's that for a come-on line?

Kids at school look at us like we're easy. You know, like Indian girls are the only ones having sex. They just expect us to get pregnant. So when we have our babies at school it's, like, so what's the big deal, you guys are like that.

Your people may have thought those things about us but that's not how we saw our people. Why do we always have to hear about what others think about us?" But stereotypes play a powerful role in how society treats First Nations teen mothers. And negative stereotypes are unavoidably part of this conversation because they are not a

It's weird now that I'm a mom and out of school. I'm half native and half white and people's attitudes about that have never showed up so clear as now that I have a kid. I'm going to school and doing good for myself. When I meet some kids I went to high school with, white kids I mean, they look at my daughter and see that she's smart and well dressed and doing well and they are shocked. "Oh, look at you," they say, "you're really doing well." What they mean is that they never thought I would ever make anything out of myself. And they look at my kid as if she should be all backward or something. But when I'm with my native cousins they just expect me to succeed. It's the weirdest thing. I'm half white so of course my kid is supposed to be smart, I'm supposed to get educated and get a job. We got the weirdest way of looking at each other and I get both sides of it.

thing of the past. The young women we spoke with contend with negative attitudes toward them every day.

Common attitudes that they have all confronted include that First Nations young women are incompetent and substandard mothers, that they are more fertile, that they consume more drugs and alcohol, and that they all come from sexually abusive and broken families. They have also heard that First Nations young men want only one thing, and that it's a tradition to have babies young. When these young women were pregnant, people would often stare or openly comment on how young they looked and make their nasty remarks loud enough to be heard.

The experience on reserve was different, but not necessarily easier. Pregnant teenagers are nothing new—a stereotype of its own. The level of acceptance made it easier for them to walk up the street on the reserve, but it didn't make them feel any better about themselves. When everyone seems to have low expectations of them, they end up having low expectations of themselves.

In his book *Prison of Grass*, Metis writer Howard Adams says that First Nations and Metis people have a "colonized personality." By this he means they believe they can never be good enough. Adams considers that it is no use for First Nations to struggle to improve their image; they weren't the ones who created it in the first place. The danger of the image is that they acquiesce to it and tell each other, "That's the way it's always been. That's the way it'll always be."

A First Nations grandmother and health worker similarly told us how negative stereotypes are a burden for the young people in her community: "Our young people see adults with their heads down. They know how we're looked on by people in town. Then pretty soon they all have their heads down. And when you're a young person and you have your head down and you feel bad about yourself then you don't think there's any future for you. You just keep your head down. It's like it has become a group thing. They all think there's no future for them other than to get together and shack up and then they get pregnant once maybe two times before they are twenty."

Everyone was doing something. Kids were drinking and smoking dope. Lots of girls my age [fifteen] were having sex. Lots of them were having a lot more sex than I was. But I got caught. It's not fair. I didn't party. I wasn't wild at all. Now everyone looks at me and that's the only thing they think about. Look at her, she had sex. Look at her, she's a wild girl.

Seen from a different perspective, of course, young First Nations women are no different from any other young women. They are lively, intelligent, and beautiful. They are daughters, granddaughters, cousins, sisters, and friends. They are enthusiastic sometimes, and depressed sometimes. They have goals and dreams and hope they can accomplish them. They make good choices and bad choices. They like to shop, play soccer, eat burgers, party, and attend music concerts. They love to dance.

Although all seemed to fit the "Indian girl with baby" stereotype, the thirteen women featured in this book were difficult to pigeonhole. They were not from an identifiable subgroup of First Nations, nor did they stand out in any way from their peers. They

Maybe more of us get pregnant than other girls, but other than that there's nothing special about me. I'm pretty normal.

I didn't know much about anything [pregnancy]. But then I don't think I was any stupider than the other girls about it either.

It's just that when you are fourteen, what do you know? It's like the lottery. I wasn't any more likely to become pregnant than my friends. I wasn't even as wild as they were. I just got caught.

were not any more poor, or less parented, or more neglected than any other girl in their communities. A few of them became pregnant during a rebellious stage; most didn't. Some were from badly alcoholic and dysfunctional families; others weren't. About half of them struggled with school; the other half were good students. Several were heavy partiers; some hardly partied at all. They were, and are, just ordinary Canadian First Nations teenagers.

These young women saw themselves as typical teenagers, no different from their peers, and certainly not "bad girls." They couldn't see any particular reason why they would be more likely than their peers to become pregnant. Four of them repeated that they had been sure they would be one of the girls to make it through their teenage years without becoming a mother.

But no matter how the girls thought about themselves, they were all keenly aware of how others saw them. That's why many of them stayed inside when they were pregnant—to hide from public opinion. Some of them didn't go to the doctor because they were scared and embarrassed. Some of them rarely went to the pool to swim, or to the parks to walk, because they thought people would look at them and talk about them. Once their babies were born, many of them hardly went off the reserve at all.

One young woman with whom we spoke had thought deeply about the effects of public opinion on her baby. She said that she had noticed that people usually ogled and smiled at a baby in pub-

I roll over and wish I didn't have to get up. It's not so bad if I just have to be around the people who already know. If I stay around home it's okay. But if I have to go out and face people, like people in the public, it's hard. Every day, it seems, I have to face something new. I have to go somewhere and face more people looking at me and wondering, how old is she? There's just another pregnant Indian girl.

lic. "That's giving that baby all kinds of positive reinforcement," she said. "But when I go out with my baby people look at me and her as if we are weird—with that 'God, how old is she? Is that her baby?' look on their faces. Don't you think that's going to affect my little girl? She's already getting looked at like she's done something wrong." It wasn't herself the young woman was worried about. It was her little girl.

One of the young women interviewed for this book was a good student who became pregnant at the age of fifteen. She was angry at herself for getting pregnant in grade nine and becoming one of the Indian statistics that she so desperately wanted to avoid. She thought her pregnancy was easier for her family to accept than it was for her. But there was a practical edge to her voice when she explained how she did graduate—just two years late. She was enrolled in college and intended to earn a degree. She had resigned herself to playing a double role, that of mother and student. She believed a degree was more important than ever once she became a parent; it was simply going to take longer. But she also felt that she was not doing a great job at either mothering or being a student. High school was one thing. She brought her baby to the daycare and the teachers coached her through to graduation. College was another matter altogether. What with child care, homework, and dating a new boyfriend, she never had time for anything and she feared her son spent too much time away from her. She didn't know how to settle down to all her responsibilities, and she wasn't getting the family help for which she had hoped. Her mother had returned to school, and her sister was also a single mother struggling to attend college. While her family accepted her baby in principle, in practice there were few people who had time to help her. Despite the fact that nothing had turned out the way she had planned, she still intended to complete her goal.

This young woman's experience was not uncommon. Another young woman was an A student, who was placed in advanced classes and expected to be accepted directly into the university of her choice once she graduated. When she became pregnant in grade ten her family was disappointed in her for a few days, but she was devastated. She had had high hopes for herself when she was young, but before she became pregnant she had started to fool around and miss classes. She said she'd felt out of place in the accelerated classes because she was the only First Nations person and the other kids excluded her from their group.

I knew lots of girls who got pregnant but I sure didn't think I was going to. It's not like I planned it or anything. I figured I'd finish school, get a career, the whole thing. The way my mom talked about girls getting pregnant, like you better not, I honestly thought it wouldn't happen to me.

But it was her own peers that really got to her. They made fun of her for wanting to be smart and eventually "Who do you think you are?" got too hard to take. She started missing classes and pretty soon her grades plummeted. She fit in to her First Nations peer group, got pregnant, quit school, and became a stay-at-home mother until her relationship ended. Since then she's finished high school, and tried to attend college, but she can't settle down. She hopes that by the time her daughter is in school she will have her plans of becoming a lawyer back on track. But not only is she carrying the double burden of wanting to fulfill her dreams and wanting to be the best mother she can be, she is still a teenager and can't stop herself from acting like one. The breaks she gets when her family looks after her baby don't give her time to get her life together; they give her only enough time to go out and be a teenager.

My family had such high expectations of me. I was going to finish school, go to college, and become somebody. I know how much First Nations people need to succeed. I was going to be one of those successes. There is twice as much pressure on good First Nations students. It's like you are doing this for all of us. Shit, I felt that pressure all my life. You are going to be one of the few that make it. I still will. It's just that it's going to take me longer now I have a kid. I took a couple of extra years to graduate. I went to college for a while but it was too hard with baby. My dreams aren't going to happen when I had hoped, but I will get through it.

Modern First Nations young women live in a lag time between old values and new expectations. Kim Anderson writes, "At one time there was a reverence for mothers and motherhood, and recognition of woman's power as the root of the family, community, and Nation. These notions and ideals are still part of our collective psyche, providing a sense that, as women, it is part of our 'roles and responsibilities,' our purpose, as it were, to have children." Yet, while women's power is still the root of the family and community, the community structure that once recognized their power has changed. What's left of the old way is a deep belief that a woman's purpose is to have children, and what is missing is the support that mothers need, especially when they are teen-agers.

All of these thirteen modern young women agreed with Anderson. "First Nations women believe in having children," one young woman said. "That's our role. It's just that having a baby so young is extra hard. And these days it's not like it used to be. There's so much else going on." Like First Nations women of the past, they believed that having children was their primary role as a woman. Even after getting pregnant, none of them questioned whether or not they wanted to be a mother. Now their job is to accomplish something that has never been done in their communities—they are the first generation to combine mothering with education and a career.

3

WE NEED TO UNDERSTAND

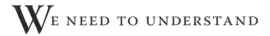

"Sex, these days," the girl's grandmother says. "It's every-where. When I was a girl you didn't see all this sex on TV; we didn't even have TV. What's a kid supposed to do?"

The girl waits eagerly for her grandmother to continue, but that's all she says. Yeah, the girl thinks, what's a kid sup-posed to do? She wants to ask her grandmother to tell her more but she doesn't want to appear too interested, either. She is only twelve and she knows one thing for sure, and that is her grandmother will say she's too young to be thinking about such things.

But sex is everywhere. The girl has seen full-out inter-course on TV, her boyfriend always talks about doing it, and she knows her older cousin has already gone all the way. The girl has kissed boys before but that was it until the night before. It was the first time a boy put his hands down her shirt. Her boyfriend even tried getting them down her pants. She was happy the waist of her jeans was too tight, but he kept trying until his brother walked into the room.

The girl had been excited at first. She liked how it felt with his hands exploring her body, but then she got scared.

When would he quit? What would he do next? What if he hadn't been interrupted?

The girl has heard about condoms. Hasn't everybody? The guy is supposed to use one, right? But she doesn't have one, and even if she did she wouldn't know what to do with one. She's never even seen one for real. Just the thought of asking her boyfriend to put one on makes her feel dumb. And when she really lets the thought of his thing come into her mind, at first she feels all tingly and curious but then she feels gross. What is she supposed to do with it?

If only someone would talk to her so she wouldn't have to bring the subject up herself. She tries to get the words out: "Grandma, what is a kid supposed to do?" But she is too embarrassed so she goes to her room.

The young women we talked to said they learned about sex, relationships, and becoming a woman from television, talk shows, their friends, their boyfriends, magazines, advertising, bus notices, and school—you name it, anywhere but at home. Only two of them could describe family values or community teachings that related to sex and relationships. The same two women were the only ones of the thirteen who said they had had meaningful discussions with any of their relatives about family beliefs, values, and lifestyle choices that had to do with sexuality or relationships.

On a bus is not where you would normally expect to obtain information about sex and birth control, but that's where one young mother said she learned pretty much all she knew about the subject. One Saturday when she was thirteen or fourteen years old, and before she became pregnant, she and her friends took the bus to a mall and she noticed an advertisement above the back window. It was a flashy blurb about birth control and safe sex. Each time she caught the bus after that, she looked at the advertisement. After a while she realized that every couple of weeks the advertisement changed. She eagerly anticipated reading the latest instalment. She had so many unanswered questions, and she hoped each week that the advertisement might answer them for her.

But the advertisements simply raised more questions in her mind than they answered. In frustration, she then picked up every pamphlet on safe sex and birth control that she found in

I'm glad I had some time going to church when I lived with my grandma. I got some stuff there about not having sex and not doing drugs and stuff. It kept me straight for a while. At least I got something about what my grandma believed in. I don't have a clue about the rest of my family.

her doctor's office and school medical room, and read them all front to back. She definitely did not want to become a teen mother. The trouble was, she said, that the information she read didn't always make sense, she didn't know how to apply it to her own life, and she didn't know anyone she could talk to about it. Fundamentally, the brochures may have covered all the technical details, but they didn't deal with the complex emotional decision of whether or not to have sex in the first place—at least, not in any way she could usefully employ. She knew the details about intercourse and birth control, but she didn't know whether she wanted to have sex. She didn't have a condom to use, and she said that even if she had, she wouldn't have known what to say about it to her boyfriend anyway.

When advertising culture or mass media act as the principal purveyors of personal, intimate, and complex information, neither can assess whether a young person understands what has been said or how he or she feels about it. The media disseminate raw bits of information in "sound bites" that are not set in any personal context, and are frequently glamorized. The message arrives from the outside and superimposes ideas of lifestyle on young people. These images are often incongruent with the real-life circumstances of

It's like all that stuff out there about sex and guys and relationships, it makes it all look so great. That's all you see. It's like that's all life's about. I wish someone had told me different. I wish I had spent more time with my girlfriends and played more sports and done more things like dancing. No one told me any different. No one encouraged me to do other stuff.

It's kind of weird because sex is everywhere. Hell, you see it on TV all the time. Everyone jokes about it but you can't talk about it seriously because you're too embarrassed. That's crazy.

youth and often assume far too much knowledge or sophistication on the part of the reader or observer.

The young woman on the bus, for example, could understand that the advertisement she was reading said that it was okay to say no to sex. But it failed to give her any basis for saying no. Since no one had taught her why she could say yes or no, she just assumed everyone had sex sooner or later, some better prepared with birth control than others. But in the absence of family or community teachings that provided reasons for her actions, it was difficult for her to incorporate the intimate but limited information provided by the advertisements and brochures into her life, and apply it meaningfully.

The young women wanted and needed more than bus advertisements. They wanted to learn what sorts of things work and what don't work and why, from people they know who have experienced these things and to whom they can relate in the context of their own lives. They wanted to talk to adults and they wanted those adults to listen and respond. They all said that the adults in their lives didn't talk to them enough, especially about personal things, and that most adults didn't listen very well. Knowledge about sexuality and relationships apparently is not currently being transferred from one generation to the next, at least not sufficiently to fill the gaping knowledge vacuum that exists.

The focus groups provided the young women with a safe environment to freely share their stories. They clearly felt the strength that came from communicating not only with their peers but with the facilitators as well. After one young woman said that she didn't want to have sex with her boyfriend but gave in after his constant pressure, the other girls began to discuss how hard it was for them to keep up to their partners' sexual demands. Before long they were talking about what they liked and what they didn't like about sex and how to respond to their own feelings and to their boyfriends' requests.

Although high school sex educators have the information about sexually transmitted infections and birth control that young people desperately need, it is far from easy for them to inspire any change in thinking or habits in teenagers. Teens don't appear to listen; if they do, they don't seem to change their behaviour as a result. It cannot be assumed that just because teenagers appear to be interested in sex, it follows that they should be interested in sex education. The subject matter is embarrassing, and current delivery methods of sex education, as described by the young women in our group, are typically dry, technical, and negative. Effective sex education does not comprise just raw facts about anatomy, intercourse, contraception, and infections: it's about the whole young woman and man and the relationships they have with one another.

Whose job is it to teach young people about sexuality and birth control in a personal way? What should be said? Where should it be

Sex is, like, out there. No one questions all the crap that we see everywhere. I wish someone in my family had taught me about saying no and why to say no and stuff like that. No one told me that I had a choice. All I got told was that sex hurt and after a while it doesn't. It was, like, that's the way it is.

My auntie sat me down and said that I probably wouldn't like sex at first. Then she laughed and said it gets better. I didn't know what to say to her and that's about all anyone said to me about it.

We had sex education at school. But I don't remember most of it. It didn't seem like it was about me so I didn't listen.

Teenagers don't always look like they are listening. But that doesn't mean you don't tell them. We need to know what our parents think is right and wrong. What works and what doesn't.

People think teenagers don't want anyone to tell them stuff. But, like, how are we going to know stuff unless someone tells us?

I had a hard time in school. They would be, like, if you have any questions then just ask. I wouldn't ask. I would wait until the very end of class and then maybe say something. I got so frustrated when kids would ask right in the middle of something. I thought they were so rude.

taught, and at what age? A few years ago, a local tribal school hired a First Nations health nurse to teach sex education to grades eight and nine. She was young and hip, and unafraid to talk about sex in a way that was relevant to teenagers. The nurse talked graphically about sexual practices, anatomy, and relationships. She translated technical information into the language of teenagers, and the habits of teenagers into the language of her profession. The young women in our groups who had attended her sessions said that she was the best sex educator they had ever encountered. "She cut through the crap," they said, and talked about sex as it really was. She legitimized their feelings and experiences, wasn't afraid to talk about the details, and, most importantly, she laid out the risks in a way the young people couldn't avoid considering. They were finally getting answers to their questions and learning information that was critical to their lives and future decisions. Unfortunately, when the school board and elders heard about some of her graphic descriptions, they fired her. No one asked the young people what they thought.

To play it safe, the school then hired elders to talk to teenagers about traditional birth control practices. The young people listened, but they didn't get very much information about current birth control methods, sexually transmitted infections, or relationships in the contemporary context in which they were living. The elders talked about traditional family values and practices, and the importance of young people building a strong identity. What the elders were doing constitutes an equally important teaching practice. Their classes were laying a critical foundation of guidelines which the youth could use in making decisions. But it wasn't enough on its own—what the young women needed and wanted, they said, was *both* kinds of lessons.

Furthermore, effective sex education may not be just for teenagers. Some of the young women felt that teachers and family should have begun to talk with them about relationships and sexuality when they were eight or nine years old. By the time they had a sex education class at school at the age of thirteen or fourteen, it was much too little and far too late. They all agreed that if teachings about relationships and sexuality had been incorporated into their world in a holistic and age-appropriate way before they became sexually active, they would have been ready to listen.

Families are as responsible for sex education, of course, as the

We were taught not to ask questions to our elders. I didn't ask because I thought I might look stupid. Asking questions is disrespectful, like maybe they told me already and I wasn't listening. It's disrespectful not to listen. So I don't want to ask because I don't want to look like I wasn't listening. I don't ask anything. I watch and I listen but I don't ever ask. I think when I was growing up they said, "Shut up, I'm talking to you. Don't speak unless you are asked." Only a few people who I knew were open—then I would ask them stuff.

I just thought if I didn't know something it was because I hadn't listened. That's what my mom and grandma said all the time—listen—you just don't listen.

school system. However, few families are talking about sexuality, safe sex, or relationships with their children. The liberation of sexual practices has gone hand in hand with the assumption that young people have a right to make up their own minds, and adults shouldn't impose their ideas on them. The result is that, while adults are not imposing their ideas, everything else still is—especially the media with their hard-sell messages.

Learning at home also seems to present special challenges in First Nations families. The young women said they had been taught that they should listen to older people without responding, as an act of respect. In their world view, questioning elders

I watched and listened to what the old people said and did but mostly I learned what not to do. I watch women with their babies or with their husbands and I think, "I don't want to be like that," so I don't act that way. There aren't many people that I see as role models for me. You learn what you don't want by watching other people. I don't think that's the way it was supposed to be but that's how it works for me.

and telling them what you think shows disrespect, so if you disagreed or were confused, you kept quiet rather than risk censure—a hard tradition to live with when modern questions need to be addressed.

One young woman said she tried hard to watch and listen and she never questioned her elders, but it didn't serve her very well. She had questions that didn't get answered and she heard things she didn't understand. She said that by watching other people she learned mostly what she shouldn't do. She saw things she didn't like and learned from her mistakes (and those of others) what to avoid and what doesn't work. But then she couldn't decide what she *should* do. Although she said she was learning to find her own way and develop her own style, her trial and error method has caused her to make a lot of mistakes that she could have avoided if she had more good role models and relevant information. She asked why

The only thing I remember being told was I would know what was right for me. That's it. That's all I got. How do you base a decision on that? How was I going to know what was right for me? What did I know about right and wrong? I wish I knew then what I'm learning now. Getting into sex changed my life and I didn't know that before. Why doesn't someone tell us?

older people aren't just more straight-forward about stuff like sex and rela-tionships, adding that it would sure be a lot easier on young people.

Regardless of the source, relevance in sex education is critical. It requires including the entire story: not just the technical framework and not just vague platitudes about doing what's right. The young women said they got bored with generalized statements about what is good for them or what isn't. And they didn't want just the bad news, either. They wanted to talk about their real-life circumstances and experiences. They wanted to talk about what they were hearing in the media. The health nurse who had talked about the details was popular with her students because she made the subject real and relevant. She talked about the colour and scent and texture of her subject. She spoke about sex and its implications so kids could understand how her teachings applied to their lives.

Given the opportunity, the young mothers said, young people want to listen—to their peers, to their parents and family, to profes-sionals, to anyone who will talk to them and help them learn. They also want someone to listen. How will we know, they asked, unless someone tells us? And how will adults know what is going on with us unless we tell them?

4

Sex Changes Everything

The girl plops on the bed and looks in the mirror sitting on the dresser. She sees a girl with no makeup, a puffy face, and her hair falling out of a ponytail. Sloppy. That's the word that comes to mind. And putting on weight, that's the other thing that comes to mind. Bored, stuck, bossed around, trapped, old married lady, knocked up—all these words come into her head.

She remembers the first time she sat on her boyfriend's bed and looked in the same mirror. Her makeup was perfect, her jeans a size four and skin-tight. Hot. That was the word that came to mind the first time she had sex with her boyfriend. She remembers how excited she was and how much she wanted to please him. She remembers how much she wanted to have sex—it all sounded so great.

"Hold on a minute," her boyfriend shouts from the other room. "I'll be right there."

He wanted her in the bedroom a few minutes ago; now he's talking to his cousin and expects her to wait.

She pulls the elastic out of her hair and lets it fall helter-skelter over her face. She sticks her tongue out at the mirror as if to say "Up yours."

Why wait? *she thinks.* Why not just walk out? Why am I sticking around here with him? He doesn't even act like he likes me anymore. And I don't really like him much, either.

Having sex wrecked everything. As soon as they had sex her boyfriend started to act like he owned her and now sex is all they ever do. She hates it, but she said yes once—how can she turn him down now? And on top of everything else, she's missed her period and is gaining weight. She doesn't even want to think about how she might be pregnant.

She combs her fingers through her silky black hair and then lifts it into a loose bun at the back of her head. She tucks the untied strands behind her ear. She stands up and rear-ranges her jeans on her hips and lifts her T-shirt to show a thin slice of belly. She smiles at herself smiling back at her.

"You look good, girl," she says out loud. "Now walk right out that door and then right on out the front door and down the driveway. Don't stop until you're . . ."

Her boyfriend walks in before she finishes her sentence.

"Who you talking to?" he asks.

"No one," the girl answers.

"You're crazy but you look good," he says.

"Thanks."

He gives her a gentle push and she falls back on the bed. She likes looking good and she likes it when he notices. For now, she forgets the door and the driveway.

When we asked the young mothers why they became pregnant, most of them said what we had expected—the condom came off, we didn't use any birth control, I forgot to take my birth control pills. But then one young woman said that her pregnancy was simply the result of having sex; it wasn't about birth control at all. Others had similar responses. "Getting pregnant, having a baby, is just about having sex," said one of them. "It's no more complicated than that. It's not like you're making some big choice or something. I never thought about sex as a choice. It's just something that happens to you."

Her passive response, and others like it, was disturbing. Does it follow that pregnancy is something that just happens along with sex? Having a baby just happens? Why didn't these young women feel as though they had control over their bodies' reproduction?

More than a generation ago, sex did equal pregnancy, at least for some. Prevention (when those over about age fifty were teenagers) meant abstinence, withdrawal, or fitting sex into "safe" windows of time based on the loose calculation of the menstrual cycle and a certain element of hoping for the best. When unreliable prevention methods failed, the girl had a baby unless she had access to a clandestine abortionist and desired that option. But in today's climate of choice for

I was never told about sex or anything. I didn't know what to think about sex. After the first time I did it I thought I didn't want to do it anymore.

I was twelve when I started having sex. That was when my mom was drinking a lot and there were always guys around the house. I thought it was all right because that's when I started drinking. I was just kind of there. I wasn't on birth control. I don't know how I didn't get pregnant right away.

I just got so I didn't care. I did what everyone else did. I hated sex but I just did it to keep people happy. It had a lot to do with guys just taking advantage of me because I was drinking and I was so young. Sex is not that good. I don't really like it.

modern women, it is difficult to accept that some women, young as they are, do not yet realize that they can say no.

Birth control is easily available. Abortions are available for the most part on demand, and free of charge. But whether it is simply a matter of choice, or a failure to use effective birth control or

For most of us sex isn't, like, the biggest thing. In fact having sex isn't a big thing at all. It's the consequences that really mess up your life. But you don't think of things like that when you're fourteen or fifteen. It's just not a fourteen-year-old thing to be doing—thinking of the long-term consequences of your life.

take advantage of termination options, for young First Nations women the disquieting reality appears to be that many simply accept their fate passively. "That's what happens to us" and "that's what happens to everyone" attitudes set the bar low for young people in the community. Although these young women had wanted something very different for themselves, and may not be happy about aspects of their lives, they still seemed complacent about them. Even when it came to sex, birth control, relationships, and pregnancy, most of them were astoundingly indifferent.

"Why did you choose to have sex?" was not a question we had initially planned to ask for the purposes of this conversation. We had planned to concentrate on four main themes: pregnancy, choosing to have the baby, choosing to keep the baby, and mothering the baby. Why they got pregnant, we thought, was related to birth control. Why they chose to have the baby was related to a decision not to have an abortion. Choosing to keep the baby had to do with not putting it up for adoption. The last theme was about parenting. But almost immediately, we realized that asking about their choice to have sex in the first place had to be the starting point for the discussion.

At first, it seemed like a moot point to the young women. "What do you mean, why did we choose to have sex?" they asked. It did not take long, however, before they realized we were not asking some grand moral question so much as one that had to do with their personal circumstances. It was not necessarily a question they had ever asked themselves previously. As a result, they also started asking themselves some interesting additional questions: Why did I have sex with *him* in particular? Why did I have sex *when* I did? Did I even consciously choose to have sex? Did I enjoy it? Just because I had sex once, does that mean I have to keep doing it?

Sex, in youth culture, is assumed; it is explicit and implicit in everything young people encounter and do. In today's society, that means, for example, that underwear is part of the costume; pubic hair is shaved so the jean line can drop; full frontal nudity is shown on prime-time television; and everything is discussed in full, bold, raunchy colour any time of the day. If television is to be believed, everyone is having sex all the time.

Conservative Canadian estimates are that 57 percent of young men and 54 percent of young women become sexually active between the ages of fifteen and nineteen. Fifteen is the average age for young women to become sexually active. One source estimates that 35 percent of American teenage girls have been pregnant at least once before they turn twenty.

Previous generations believed that sex before marriage was a sin. In the same way that sex is an accepted part of today's youth culture, the prohibition of sex until you were married was part of the culture that older people grew up in. It wasn't necessarily a lesson that was specifically hammered into youth, given the discomfort previous generations had in talking about sex; more usually, it was a generally accepted and indirectly absorbed principle. A male friend from

We weren't taught anything about not having sex. It seems like everyone is doing everyone.

At least in this group we talk about sex like it's just another subject. I've never done that before. I've never got to talk about what it's like for me without being laughed at. Why can't we talk like this about it—like it's normal?

No one taught me much about having sex. My cousin told me not to do it until I wanted to but I never wanted to. My boyfriend just kept pestering me about it. It was all he talked about. I wanted to try it. So I finally gave in. My boyfriend likes it a lot more than I do.

I wish I had been told to wait. No one ever said anything about waiting until you are older. If I hadn't started to have sex so young I might not have got all stuck on my boyfriend and maybe could have had more time to do other stuff. At first I even quit playing soccer. It was, like, him and me, that's it. And most of what we did was in the bedroom.

a local First Nations community, about age fifty, said he knew growing up that sex before marriage was wrong. But he could not recall being directly taught that premarital sex was bad. Instead, the lesson was always implied. "Whenever I had a girlfriend, they told me she was my cousin," he said, chuckling at the memory. "It didn't matter how distant a relation she was to us. My dad or mom took me aside and said, 'You can't date her, she is related to you.' Every girl I was attracted to became my relation. They wouldn't let me date anyone. Mom used to chase the girls off the beach so they wouldn't come around looking for me and my brothers."

His parents didn't sit the boys down and tell them they couldn't have sex before marriage; they simply constructed barriers to prevent the young people from getting together. That behaviour was not exclusive to First Nations, by any means. Neither Aboriginal nor non-Aboriginal cultures spoke directly to the prohibition, but both had taboos around sex for the young. The silence that fell on the room when topics related to sex were brought up was usually enough to let young people know it was a subject that was out of bounds. In those days, of course, there were no television programs or movies or Internet sites to tell youth anything else.

Some things do not appear to have changed. Like the previous generation, the parents of most of the young women never said anything directly prohibiting youth sex, let alone about sex in general. But in the contemporary climate of youth culture, the young women were unaware of any social barriers to having sex at an early age. Only one young woman said she vaguely thought sex was wrong for young, unattached people, although she didn't really know why. The others thought sex was something you just did sooner or later, with no constraints other than pregnancy or disease. Sex was anything but a taboo in their homes. Many of them were free to sleep with their boyfriends in their family's home, with no parental guidance on the implications of becoming sexually active.

We got that birth control stuff at school, but it was mostly about how you get pregnant and your body and stuff; it wasn't about making decisions.

As noted in the previous chapter, the young women did receive basic physical sex information from school sex education classes. They knew how pregnancy occurred, and understood simple information about intercourse and sexually transmitted diseases. They said that when they got pregnant they had a vague knowledge of their anatomy and how their bodies functioned internally. But they had no idea what it meant emotionally or mentally to become a woman, or how to have a healthy relationship.

Most significantly, they didn't know how to make decisions about sex. In fact, it wasn't until they talked about it together in the context of this research project that most of them realized that having sex actually was a decision. When confronted with having sex, most of them couldn't think of any reason not to do it. They had no lessons to draw upon, no prohibitions, and no warning bells sounding: Am I ready for this? Is this the right time? Is this the right guy? Is this what I want? Some of the young women thought briefly and remotely about pregnancy and sexually transmitted diseases, but those worries seemed only hazy possibilities that happened to other people. They didn't have a significant impact on their behaviour.

One young woman resisted her boyfriend for as long as she could, but only because sex didn't appeal to her. After a few weeks, his constant begging got the best of her and she thought she might as well give him what he wanted in order to shut him up. She had come to believe it was going to happen sooner or later anyway. Giving in was simple enough. The aftermath, however, was far more

I wasn't into sex at all. I did it for my boyfriend. We were together for a couple of years and seriously I thought I had some kind of deficiency. I just wasn't into it. Mostly I thought it was gross. Now I'm older and I was with an older guy and I realize, what do you know when you are a kid? It just wasn't the thing for me when I was young.

complicated. Once she started having sex with him, that's all he wanted to do. Sex became a way of life for her. The young couple spent more time in the bedroom than doing anything else. "I wouldn't have given in if I'd known how it was going to turn out," she said. "After I had sex once I could have lived without it. But my boyfriend wouldn't let up. Once we had sex it was, like, we're doing it now so I could never say no again."

Most of the others, however, were sexually curious. They had no reason to wait or say no. But they too hadn't thought much about the consequences of saying yes. One young woman didn't think sex was something that needed much thought—she just fell into it. Once she had done it for the first time, she thought it was something you just kept doing whether you wanted to or not. When asked if sex was pleasurable for her, she hesitated and replied, "Not really."

Sexual curiosity, of course, occurs independently of the emotional and intellectual maturity to handle the consequences of having sex, a disconnect that is a significant factor in making poor decisions. But the young women's apparent indifference to sexual decision making also reflects the community's lack of clearly defined and accepted beliefs and values about sexuality. Among First Nations today, traditional teachings and methods of discouraging early sexuality are rarely practiced. Nor is anything taking their place. The media have taken over as the primary source of information, and they are telling youth that sex is everywhere and gratification must be immediate. Without adequate guidance, these young women were left on their own to stumble through confusing and demanding sexual experiences without the ability to make informed choices.

Sex presented the young women with a complicated set of competing interests. They wanted to explore their emerging sexual feelings and urges. They wanted to be liked, to fit in with their friends, and to please their boyfriends. They wanted to be loved and feel needed and attached. They wanted attention. At the same time, fulfilling their own sexual needs was much more complicated than having intercourse. In order to deal with their emerging sexuality they needed to take time, set their own limits, and become familiar with their needs and desires. They needed skills and maturity they didn't have, and in a climate of sexual liberty and lack of direction, they couldn't connect their freedom of choice with any teachings or practices that might have helped them take the time they needed and make that choice well.

If I could do it again I wouldn't have sex at all. It was nothing. After all that and then finally I had it and it was, like, is that all . . .

I was all excited. We were going to have sex. So he gets on top of me and I'm, like, ouch. He's all excited and does his thing. It takes a few minutes and then he's, like, over. I'm thinking great, now he's going to be all intimate with me. I felt all close to him. And then he's getting up and pulling up his pants and he's out of there. I'm lying in bed thinking, is that it? Well, okay, but what's the big deal?

Although none of the young women described themselves in this way, they all said they knew wildly aggressive girls who chased boys until they got sex. But they also thought that most of the "wild" girls were probably seeking attention, competitively attempting to win the "hottest" guy and offering sex as a "top seller." We asked them if they thought these young women were satisfied or getting pleasure from their conquests. "Yeah," they said. "Satisfied and pleased—at least for a while—that they got the guy. Who knows about the sex?"

On top of everything else, sexual decision making for teenagers is often complicated by alcohol and drugs. Kim Anderson's study

Sex usually happens, especially at first, at parties when everyone is drinking. It's like everyone is doing it. Sometimes it's like everyone is doing it with everyone. When you're drinking it seems like it's going to be so much fun.

When you're drunk you're not thinking straight about anything. It's, like, hey, this is cool.

of urban Aboriginal youth in Ontario named substance abuse as the most common reason for teen conception. Youth are no different from adults. They are less inhibited and more careless under the influence of alcohol, and less likely to use protection. Mix drugs and alcohol with a liberal attitude to sexuality and a leniency toward pregnancy, and well-considered decisions become unlikely. This was the case for many of the young women in our focus group.

The young men are as unguided and unrestrained as the young women. Sex, for the young men we spoke with, was also something that "just happened," and not something they thought they controlled. A young woman told me about a story she had heard about a teenage girl at a party who was approached by a young man she had never met. He said to her, "I want to come in your face." The girl was dumbstruck. "What kind of pickup line is that? What's a girl supposed to say?" commented the young woman relating the story. "Where does a guy come up with a line like that?" I asked. "Porno," she said. "Where do you think?"

During a typical house party, the young women said, the young men head off to watch porn on the computer while their girlfriends hang around and visit. When the subject comes up later in conversation, they join in to please the guys. But only a few of the young women said they liked pornography and willingly joined the sex talk.

Where do boys get their ideas about sex? The young men we spoke with had a simple answer: everywhere. But pornography was their primary sex education teacher. Pornographic movies, Internet sites, and magazines are widely available. By the time many boys are twelve or thirteen, and in some cases much younger, they are able to access pornography in some form. And the scope of that pornography is only expanding. Young men have never before had access to such a steady diet of explicit material at such a young age. Studies tell us that up to 70 percent of youth aged fifteen to seventeen in the United States have looked at pornography online, and there is no reason to believe the number would be lower in Canada. An average porn site can generate as many sexual images in a minute as an entire issue of *Hustler* magazine, and the pornographic material seen online is exponentially more violent and explicit than the centrefolds of past generations.

Pornography creates high expectations in young men and puts them in immediate conflict with young women. At a time when the latter are looking for exploration, comfort, intimacy, attention, and acceptance, the former are looking to recreate the highly contrived images they have seen on their computers.

Not all young men are into pornography, but if these young women are right, a lot more are into it than local front-line workers currently think. The workers we spoke with had not previously considered it an important

I think it's really disgusting. He has to have his porn. Then after he's been watching it for a while he comes after me and he's got all these ideas in his head. I don't know what to do with him.

What the guys say:

Sex? You learn about sex from everything, don't you? Sex is everywhere.

Porn. We learn about sex in porn.

No way, man. I don't watch porn. Who needs to watch porn when you can make your own?

Yeah, man, I make my own porn.

No one taught me about sex. I get all I need to know on videos and stuff. It's all there. Everything.

The young boys are getting into porn on the computer. I see boys eleven and twelve into it. They run around talking about sex like they know what it's all about.

If you are into a good long-term relationship you might want to use porn. It's up to you. But for a young girl with no experience with sex, porn is pretty harsh.

Having sex put a lot of pressure on our relationship. I told my boyfriend, if I had my way and if I could turn back the clock I'd have never had sex. Just the word sex is a big argument. It's weird. It changes things.

aspect of teen relationships and sexuality. It's still too early for long-term studies to have addressed the issue, so there is little information available to such workers on how extended use of Internet pornography is really affecting young people.

Once the young women became sexually involved, everything in their relationships changed, and not for the better. What might have started as an exciting infatuation—the cat-and-mouse game of attraction, full of possibilities—often quickly turned possessive and controlling. They described sex as if it set off a trigger in their boyfriends, a primal response of "ownership." When one young woman and her boyfriend finally had sex, it was as if he had "claimed and conquered" her, and suddenly every other boy became a threat to him. It was as if she had instantly become a sexual being, potentially some other boy's object for sexual fulfillment, and her boyfriend became irrationally jealous.

Sex, for most of the young women, came before a trusting relationship had been established. They started having sex with their boyfriends within weeks of getting together, and only three had been with their boyfriends for more than a few months before they became pregnant. Rather than enhancing their relationships, sex messed things up. First they became pregnant, and then they were faced with trying to sexually satisfy a boyfriend they hardly knew while their bodies became bigger and uncomfortable. Once the baby was born, it became harder still.

Three of the young mothers had had a fulfilling sexual experience with their boyfriends, but only after getting to know each other and being together for a few years. As one young woman said, "After we were together for a while sex was good. I have to say we had a good sex life. He was good to me. I'm glad I was with him because I was so young. Lots of girls aren't so lucky."

The dreary truth for most of the young women was that, in spite of their freedom to experience sexual satisfaction, it seemed to have eluded them. Sexual liberty did not mean they had control over their bodies, or control over the kind of sex they engaged in. The act of sexual intercourse seemed far more like a risky habit or mating ritual gone wrong than an expression of love or experience of pleasure. It appeared overall to be neither safe, meaningful, nor satisfying. What is missing?

"It's a lack of respect," a First Nations front-line worker said, referring to the unrestrained sexual activity she heard about in her community. "If we could teach the kids to respect each other, and most of all respect themselves, then they wouldn't take advantage of each other sexually the way they do." But what does that

Relationships are hard. Once my girlfriend got with this guy she couldn't even go to the mailbox without him saying some harsh shit. Once they had sex he would not trust her one bit. Men, all they want is sex. They demand so much and if they don't get it they ask right away. If we say no then they'll just get it from somewhere else. They don't come to think we're different than them. There are times when I don't want anything to do with it. There are times when I just wish I never had sex with him in the first place because after I did it changed my whole life.

At first sex was fun. I was really into it and curious and all that. It was like we were a couple of kids playing. After a while it got like he was really demanding and I wanted to go out with our friends and stuff and he wanted to stick with me.

Sex was okay in my relationship. We waited for a while and when we did have sex we were ready for it. It was when I moved in with him that my relationship got really complicated.

Guys wait outside the bar. Shit-faced. They hang around and when we come out they say, "Hey, come on." It's like they think we're easy. It's not like they looked at us when they were sober.

respect look like? How does it play out during a party or when the kids are drunk or stoned? After watching porn on the Internet? She didn't know.

Oddly enough, the one consistent thing that all the young people said was that they *had* been taught respect. For example, one young woman said that she was taught to respect her elders. To her, that meant she should listen to what they said, because they had important knowledge. Most of the young mothers said that when they thought of respect it was in relation to their elders. But what does that have to do with sex? From the young women's perspective, having sex didn't mean a lack of respect for either themselves or their boyfriends, nor did having sex mean they lacked self-esteem. Most of them believed they respected themselves as much as any other teenager. Sex was neither a moral nor an ethical issue, nor was it an issue of self-respect or self-esteem. In fact, for most of them, having sex was a legitimate way that a young man showed he wanted his girlfriend and valued her, and therefore that he respected her.

Only one young woman said that after she became sexually active with her boyfriend he seemed to lose respect for her, and that sex seemed to be the only thing he liked about her. In a way, she believed that sex had led to disrespect; but at the same time, having sex was the only activity they did together where she felt she had any value to him. With the sole exception of violent or aggressive sex, which all of the young women strongly differentiated from "normal" sex, they couldn't equate sex with disrespect.

How can young people make sense out of sex and come to

mature, safe, and respectful decisions about how to behave? One young woman said that the trouble in her community was that "everyone was screwing everyone." Whether or not that was the case, in her mind the sexual habits of her peers and neighbours was out of control—no one needs to be married; uncles and aunts and neighbours have a series of partners without any apparent consequences or criticism. While not everyone was involved in this kind of behaviour, for this young woman perception was everything. She wanted to see respect apply to sexual relationships, and she wanted guidelines so she could see what respect looks like in action. But she didn't see such respect around her.

Once I had been with my boyfriend he didn't want me talking to anyone. He would be, like, why are you talking to him or why are you sitting over there. Then it would be, like, we would be at a party and I would be sitting on his lap and looking only at him and he would still be like that. I think it's just his insecurity. Being on the reserve everyone knows what everyone else is doing. Everyone is drinking and everyone screws around. That's what it seems like sometimes. Like, you don't really know but it's how everyone talks.

Society assumes that, aside from sexual assault, sex is a choice, and that young people can choose to have sex or not and they can choose to have it safely or not. But clearly young people don't see it that way. These young women, for example, want to know how to apply careful, subtle, and emotional consideration to having sex in ways that the young men will also understand. They want to know how to make sexual decisions, but at present they don't get a chance. Few people are talking about sex that way.

Sex education has largely become about safe sex while the other critical elements such as personal development, sense of self, need for control, the quest for intimacy, acceptance by others, and relationships are left out. It seems that families, teachers, and communities are not talking to young people about how these elements relate to sex. All of the young mothers wished they had had the opportunity to have that conversation. If someone had talked to them, they said they might have had a better idea about the jealousy, bitterness, and possessiveness that often occurs once a young couple begins to have sex. If someone had told them that they have choices about what kind of sex they could have, and where and when, they might not have passed off having sex as just another thing that happens.

Of course the young women didn't like the consequences of their actions, but they simply didn't know how to retrieve control. At the point of having sexual intercourse, fear, excitement, passion, and disgust are all present. It is not a time when a clear-headed decision is easily made, even when well-informed. But they all agreed that if they had known that sex was a choice, not a default situation, they would have wanted to make that choice, and might have made it differently. Even in a liberal sexual atmosphere, young people can believe that they have the right and responsibility to make a decision.

5

Condoms and Complications

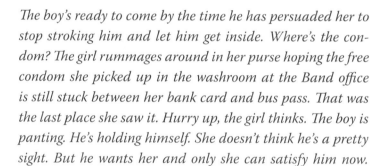

The boy's ready to come by the time he has persuaded her to stop stroking him and let him get inside. Where's the condom? The girl rummages around in her purse hoping the free condom she picked up in the washroom at the Band office is still stuck between her bank card and bus pass. That was the last place she saw it. Hurry up, the girl thinks. The boy is panting. He's holding himself. She doesn't think he's a pretty sight. But he wants her and only she can satisfy him now. She's convinced of that.

The girl bites off the corner of the package and pulls out the slippery condom. She can barely see it because the light in the bedroom is dim and her back is arched uncomfortably on top of a stack of coats tossed on the bed by partiers. The boy fumbles with his zipper, frees his penis, grabs the condom out of the girl's hand, shoves it on just in time. He pushes his stiff penis inside her. It's tough to get it in because her legs are pushed together. There isn't enough room to spread them far enough apart for comfort. The girl is dry inside and worried. It's not that the girl doesn't want the boy, it's that she thought it would be different. The girl didn't have enough time to get as excited as she thought she would be.

The girl feels a sharp pain and then a few quick and interesting sensations. After a few moments the boy collapses on top of her. They hear voices outside the door that get louder and closer. Sure that someone is going to find them there the boy jumps up, yanks up his pants, and stumbles out the door.

The girl can hear him join the voices. The boy is talking about crazy stuff, keeping the people out of the room. He's covering for her to give her time to pull her pants up. As if everyone isn't going to know what was going on.

The girl feels a damp trickle on her inner thigh. She reaches down and pulls the condom, spilling over, out of her vagina. She still feels partly stoned and partly drunk and now she is completely terrified. She drops the wet rubber onto the floor—a present for her friend's mom and dad when they get home—then shuffles out the door and rejoins the party.

She can't find the boy so she sits with the girls and shares another joint. Then she drinks another beer. The girl hopes she can forget she just played with fire. She'll have to wait to see if she is going to get burned.

The number of teenage births in Canada has dropped over the last decade, in large part because 80 percent of Canadian teenagers now use birth control methods regularly. But the picture is not the same in First Nations communities.

In Kim Anderson's study of urban Aboriginal youth in Ontario, 26 percent of the sexually active respondents said that they never used contraceptives, while another 21 percent indicated that they used it rarely, or only sometimes. Only 38 percent indicated that they always used birth control. That means that over 60 percent of sexually active urban Aboriginal youths may be at risk of contracting a sexually transmitted infection or conceiving a child with their partners. The numbers are consistent with the habits of the young people we talked to. Half of them said they used birth control, but only a few young women used it regularly.

Why, when it is so readily available and so much information is generally available about birth control, do so many of these young women fail to take full advantage of it? The young women in this book either carelessly didn't use birth control, despite fears of becoming pregnant, or their birth control did not work properly, or they didn't believe they would get pregnant so didn't think it necessary. None of them had mastered the regular habits they needed to use birth control effectively. They forgot to take their pill, they didn't understand how the birth control shot worked, the condom ripped, the condom stayed inside when the boy pulled out. Almost every young woman had a different story, but none of them were conscientious when it came to birth control.

To complicate matters, most of them didn't expect to be sexually active. Sex, especially at first, was a hit-and-miss occurrence, a spontaneous

We never thought about it. We always practised unsafe sex.

After all they say about birth control and how we need to learn about it and our bodies and all that, it just seems like when you are thirteen or fourteen there is a big gap between what you know and what you do. Sometimes you're just too young to make the right decisions anyway. There's always going to be someone who doesn't have it all together. Especially when you are just a kid.

We were young, and just too afraid to talk about birth control. Sure we learn about it at school. You know some stuff but you don't really understand how to use it for yourself. It's a lot harder when you are really out there. The stuff at school doesn't prepare you for that. And who are you going to ask?

It only happened to me once. I don't have sex that often so it's not likely to happen again. Birth control is too much trouble.

We didn't use anything at all. I just hoped I would be safe. I knew I could get pregnant but I wasn't having sex all the time or anything so I didn't think about birth control very much.

and even unexpected event. Because they didn't have sex regularly, they didn't think about birth control on a daily basis. "Why take birth control every day just to cover the few times you might actually go all the way with a boy?" they said.

In addition, despite the fact that the incidence of pregnancy from unprotected sex is as high as 85 percent, once the young women started having sex without protection, they continued to take their chances when they began to have sex regularly. The sense of invincibility common to many young people allowed the teenagers to believe that they would continue to get away with their carelessness and escape pregnancy.

One community worker said the answer to preventing teen pregnancy is to make sure every teenager has a condom in their pocket. In one way she's right: condoms are a highly effective and easily accessible means of birth control. But of course having a condom in your pocket doesn't necessarily prevent pregnancy. "By the time you get around to using the old condom stuffed in the corner of your purse," said some of the young women, "it'll probably be torn or outdated anyway. Why bother?"

Condom effectiveness is based on at least five factors: having an intact one on hand, wanting to use it, knowing how to apply it, having the experience and skill to apply it effectively, and luck. If the condom breaks, slips off, or is defective, any other skill or knowledge becomes moot. When condoms are used correctly by experienced users, they can be highly effective in preventing pregnancy. But condoms break upon use at a rate of 2 percent, up to 5 percent slip off during intercourse, and up to 13 percent slip down but not off. Fourteen out of every hundred women who use condoms as their only method of birth control become pregnant during the first year of use. As far as we could tell, no one yet has come up with the number of teenagers who become pregnant during their first year of condom use, but we are willing to bet it is higher than 14 percent.

Human error is the leading cause of condom failure, and teenagers are far more prone to making errors than adults. Teens also face special challenges in effectively using condoms. For a teenage girl to ask a young man to use a condom takes the same kind of courage and resolve as saying no to sex altogether. She must interrupt proceedings at a point at which her partner is already excited and urgent in his desires, and demand that the condom is used—a very difficult task, especially if she hardly knows the boy. Add inexperience and a cramped location into the mix, combine those factors with a young man's enthusiasm and short window of opportunity to complete the sex act, and it's easy to see why so many of the young women said that using condoms didn't work.

We never used condoms. My boyfriend wouldn't. I was so young I didn't know what I was supposed to do and he wouldn't even talk about it. I did what he said. I didn't think it would be so bad to be pregnant anyway.

We used condoms. Every time. I know exactly when I got pregnant because when we were finished the condom was broken. Sure enough I got pregnant.

It's when you are drunk that you really get into the problem. When you party and get crazy. If there wasn't all the drinking around, all the screwing around wouldn't happen so often.

But it's when young people are under the influence of drugs and alcohol that condoms become particularly ineffective. Teenagers are less likely to use condoms at all when they are drunk or stoned. When they do use them, the condoms are often carelessly handled and applied. A false sense of security has already been instilled by

If you ask me, youth leaders and health workers need to get the message to the guys. They got to start thinking about stuff like relationships and sex and birth control and taking responsibility for their babies when they get them. The guys just do their thing and then screw off if they feel like it.

Guys should have to have lessons or something. Mandatory. It would make it easier for us. I know when it comes right down to it I have to take care of myself, but it sure would help if they were a little more responsible.

It's my body and when it gets right down to it no one is going to care about it as much as me. I don't expect anyone else to take care of me even though I wish guys could have some pill or magic potion that would take care of everything. I have to take care of myself.

information on the packaging or delivered in sex education classes, to the effect that the condoms provide far greater protection than experience may actually bear out.

Interestingly, when we first started talking about birth control, the young women thought young men should be the ones to take responsibility for preventing pregnancy. Young men are thinking about sex all the time, was their argument, so they should be ready to use birth control all the time. It seemed like an easy and obvious solution. But after exploring the idea more deeply, they unanimously agreed that, while young men should take more responsibility for birth control, in the end young women are the ones who are responsible for their own bodies. They concluded that they couldn't expect anyone else to take care of them if they were not willing to take care of themselves.

They did of course want the young men to take birth control more seriously, but their priority was their own personal responsibility. That view may seem compromising. But from their point of view, the young men were simply not dependable, and pretending that they were was fraught with risk. That, however, leaves no one to bring pressure to bear on the young men and demand that they take more responsibility.

The young men we spoke to said that they knew they should be responsible for birth control, but acknowledged it didn't always happen. There were barriers from their perspective as well. Most of the young men believed that the birth control pill and shot had negative side effects for women, and they didn't want their girlfriends risking their health. Condoms were the only birth control method they thought was safe, but even so most of them didn't believe they were very effective. In fact, the young men did not have a high degree of trust in any birth control method. There was also a disconnect between what the young men said they wanted to do, and what they did—their habits did not live up to their words.

Getting the message of sexual decision making, relationship responsibility, and safe sex across to young men is a difficult task. According to the front-line workers we talked to, young men generally don't listen very well when it comes to birth control and relationships. Talking about feelings and responsibilities is a foreign experience for most teenage boys. The young men in our focus group said it helps if the messenger is "cool"—teaching

I wasn't the kind of person to take a pill every day. I kept forgetting so I decided that I would go with the shot. So I went in, got my first shot, and then you are supposed to go every three or four months, something like that. But it was such a long time after the first shot I completely forgot. When I realized I should go get another shot I went to the doctor and he asked if I could be pregnant. I said yes. So I got a pregnancy test and it was too late for the second shot.

Hey, the thing about birth control is that you have to think about it. You know, like every month or every day or every time you have sex you have to be organized. That doesn't happen with very many fourteen-year-olds. You just aren't all that put together at that age.

71

Birth control isn't safe. There are a lot of side effects and I don't trust it. I was too scared to use it. So I didn't use anything at all. Now I use an IUD. It seems to work and the doctor says it's safe. I hope so.

I'm not going to feel like crap every day just in case some day I might have sex—especially if I'm not having sex very often. Just watch the advertisements on TV. They list all the side effects of birth control pills. Those things are dangerous.

birth control to young men works better when the message is delivered by young adult men whom they look up to.

While condoms were the most common form of birth control used, the young women's use of other methods of contraception was equally hit-and-miss. A few said they briefly used birth control pills, but kept forgetting to take them. They had the same problem with the birth control shot. In fact, it was easier to remember to take a pill every day than to remember to get a shot once every three months. Only one young woman used an intrauterine device, or IUD. Ironically, that was the only birth control method any of them believed would be effective, although they didn't like the idea of having a device placed "permanently" in their bodies, and they had heard of frightening side effects. None of them had used the "morning after" pill, although they had all heard about it.

Side effects were a major concern. Those who used birth control pills or the shot experienced negative effects such as weight gain, pain, nausea, lethargy, and fatigue. Because most of them had only a cursory knowledge of the pros and cons of birth control and pregnancy, many of them decided that they were better off taking their chances or even becoming pregnant.

Unfortunately, the young women's laissez-faire attitude toward contraceptives extended to disease, fear of which did not provide them much additional incentive to use condoms. Except for AIDS, they were surprisingly untroubled by the risks of sexually transmitted infections—or they didn't believe a disease was something that could really happen to them.

When you are young you don't think all that much about diseases. They're in the back of your mind, like when you hear something on TV or something. But it's not like you're thinking you are going to get something. When I was really young I just figured that diseases were just one of those things I couldn't do much about—except hope I didn't catch something. Sometimes I got pretty freaked, especially about AIDS, but then I just thought about something else.

Fear of pregnancy appears to have been no deterrent, either, despite the fact that the young women saw evidence of pregnancy happening to other people their age and didn't particularly wish to follow suit. Only two of them were in any way inclined to becoming a mother at the time of their pregnancy. In general, it is an effective deterrent in non-Aboriginal society; why then is that not the case here? Perhaps because from their perspective, for reasons that have already been discussed, pregnancy is not the worst thing that can happen—it has become almost normal.

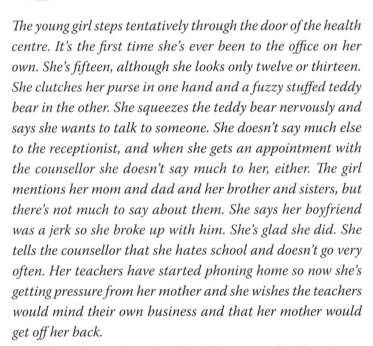

6

KEEPING THE BABY

The young girl steps tentatively through the door of the health centre. It's the first time she's ever been to the office on her own. She's fifteen, although she looks only twelve or thirteen. She clutches her purse in one hand and a fuzzy stuffed teddy bear in the other. She squeezes the teddy bear nervously and says she wants to talk to someone. She doesn't say much else to the receptionist, and when she gets an appointment with the counsellor she doesn't say much to her, either. The girl mentions her mom and dad and her brother and sisters, but there's not much to say about them. She says her boyfriend was a jerk so she broke up with him. She's glad she did. She tells the counsellor that she hates school and doesn't go very often. Her teachers have started phoning home so now she's getting pressure from her mother and she wishes the teachers would mind their own business and that her mother would get off her back.

After a few sessions the girl tells the counsellor that she got pregnant after she had been with her boyfriend for a couple of months. He didn't treat her any good and she was scared of what her mom and dad would say so early one morning, she remembers it was raining out, her boyfriend drove her to the hospital and she had an abortion. She doesn't remember much about it. Her boyfriend told her that if she didn't have an abortion he would tell everyone that she'd been fooling around. The abortion itself is a blur in her mind, but it hurt later and she still gets pains in her stomach. Maybe she has some kind of infection, she says, because the pain gets so bad sometimes she buckles over and has to sit down. But the doctor says nothing's wrong with her insides, maybe it's in her head. Now her boyfriend's gone she feels really lonely and afraid. She hears what people say about abortion and she knows she has murdered her own baby.

The girl says she can't sleep at night. She is sure something will happen to her for killing the baby, so she tries to keep her eyes open. Then when it gets really dark in her room she can hear her baby crying. It's a baby girl and she wants her mommy. The girl can feel the baby in the room with her so she holds onto the teddy bear so the baby can have something to play with. She never lets go of the teddy bear.

The girl wants her baby to know she is sorry.

At a workshop for First Nations high school students, we asked a group of teenage girls why they thought so many Aboriginal teenagers have babies compared to non-Aboriginal girls. One young woman responded immediately: "Because we don't look down on people who have babies. We accept babies, no matter what." The rest of the girls around the table nodded in agreement. But one girl interjected,

Some girls I knew had abortions and I didn't. That's the main thing you're looking at here. We're sitting here as a group of teenage moms. We're the ones who didn't have abortions. The white girls at school? I bet lots of them have had abortions— at least you hear about it.

I know in my family it wouldn't be allowed. Even if they are disappointed with you for getting pregnant they wouldn't approve of you having an abortion.

In my boyfriend's family they wouldn't approve of it either. I know I don't. I wouldn't have an abortion—I wouldn't even think about it the first time.

Now that I think about it, if I got pregnant again I would have to think about it different. But I would have real trouble doing it. I don't know if when I got to the place whether I would really be able to do it.

"Because we don't believe in abortions. It's murder."

When the male high school students were asked what they would do if their girlfriends wanted to have an abortion, each boy initially said that he would support his girlfriend's decision. Finally, however, one self-conscious boy said he thought abortion was murder, and he wouldn't want his girlfriend murdering his baby. The mood in the room changed almost immediately. By the end of the discussion, not one boy was saying that he felt comfortable with the idea of abortion.

Abortion was a complex and confusing issue for the young women in this conversation. Cultural values outside First Nations communities support abortion as a good option for a pregnant teenager. Women have fought long and hard for abortion rights so that teenage girls could have the freedom to finish school and get a job before they become mothers. On the one hand, these young women supported that principle. They wanted to be free to be a teenager, finish their education, get a good job, and, especially, avoid becoming another "Indian statistic." On the other hand, once they became pregnant, the idea of abortion was immediately objectionable.

As noted in the previous chapter, the rate of teen births has dropped in Canada, partly owing to increased use of birth control. The availability of legal abortions is another significant factor. Fifty-four percent of all teenage pregnancies in British Columbia now end in abortion. There are no statistics that indicate how many

First Nations teen pregnancies end in abortion, but in Kim Anderson's study of urban Aboriginal youth in Ontario, only 20 percent of those interviewed said that they would have one. Another 26 percent said they would have an abortion only under certain circumstances, such as rape. Abortion is simply not as well accepted on reserve as it is elsewhere: by contrast to the general statistics, nowhere near 54 percent of teen pregnancies in First Nations communities end in abortion.

It's murder. That's what I think about abortion. I feel so sad when I hear girls say they would have abortions. I feel like crying. I don't see how people can think about aborting something that will hold your hand and look at you and smile and call you Mom and depend on you. That baby is depending on you—how can you kill it?

The issue for the young women was their deeply rooted belief that abortion is murder, with specific cultural consequences. Almost all the young women said that they believed as did their families—that life begins at conception. They also believed that it does not end with abortion. Life, for the young women, was not confined to tangible and visible bodies, or restricted to firmly established moments of beginning and end. In their world view the spirit of an aborted fetus will live on and linger around the mother and the people close to her. The young women said they believed that the spirits of aborted babies would be angry and scared, and could come back and hurt the mother and father or other family members. It also might come back to life as a future baby in the family. The consequences of that were uncertain.

Most of the young women weren't certain how the details of the spirit world worked, but they were convinced of the fact that a fetus contains life, and that when an abortion occurs it is murder of a baby's body but not the end of its spirit's "life." They spoke about "having to look over their shoulder for the rest of their lives," and worrying immensely about what was going to happen if they ever aborted a baby.

It goes back to that one story where the couple had an abortion. I heard it from my children's auntie. It's supposed to be about her brother-in-law or someone. I'm not sure but I think everyone has a story like this. They weren't ready for a baby so they had an abortion. When she got pregnant again they had another abortion. Then they finally had a child and kept him. He was really off the wall. He cried and screamed when he was a baby and then when he got older he was really mean to his parents. Finally his mom asked him what was wrong with him. He said, "I kept trying to come and you kept sending me back to the other side." He said that to his parents, and that sticks to me.

It was scary. Like when a friend was telling me, "You won't believe who just miscarried a baby." Then she said, "Her baby knew she had an abortion already so it's not going to come."

"That's our belief exactly," an elder said when I told her the story one young woman had recounted (see quotation), about the screaming child of a mother who'd previously had abortions. "If you take a life, it could come back and get you in some way. You will lose something if you take something. The old people taught that if you take that life then you will have to suffer for it sometime. Maybe later. You never know when. Someone in your family might be taken from you. Or you might get sick. Or your actions could hurt someone else in your family. They may get sick because of you. You have to be careful and watch out."

When discussing this with a non-Aboriginal public health nurse, her response was "Oh my God, don't they know that abortions are their right?" But for them, abortion was not a question of rights. It was about life and death—a matter for First Nations spiritual leaders and the First Nations population to examine. Regardless of any legal rights, only they can decide how to reconcile the dissonance that occurs in young women between belief and practice when they have an abortion.

Their world view comes at a cost. When they become pregnant, Aboriginal young women are forced to decide between betraying their values and having a baby that they may not be able to care for, even if they want to. Some of the young women in our groups had had an abortion and others admitted that if their life became so unmanageable that they couldn't provide a decent life for another baby, or if they were raped, they would consider having an abortion. But they also thought that they would have a hard time living with a decision to terminate the life of a child. Half of them, however, said they would not have an abortion under any circumstances. Motherhood is not a choice under those conditions, but simply inevitable.

The young women said that friends they knew who did have an abortion can't talk to their mothers and grandmothers, or even their friends. One young woman who became pregnant at fifteen and didn't want to face motherhood said she thought long and hard about her options and then said, "Mom, what would you think if I had an abortion?" Her mother broke into tears and replied, "You can't kill my grand-

I think that's why there are so many First Nations girls who have babies and can't look after them properly. White girls would have an abortion. We don't. We at least have that first baby because we are so afraid of abortion. We know abortion is wrong. So whether we can look after our baby or not we have it. Some girls have two or three babies, not because they want them, but because they won't have an abortion.

If there isn't anything else you can do then it's your last option. My family and friends don't like it much. I have two friends that have had abortions and it's really, really hard for them. They haven't forgiven themselves for it yet. I just don't think it's the right thing to do. I think it is cruel. It stays with the girls around here for a long time. The girls are really young and really scared. They just keep their pregnancy a secret, and then they don't have abortions and they keep drinking because of their secret.

child." The young woman was horrified with herself for even thinking of abortion. When she thought more about it, she decided that she too believed that her child was already part of her extended family. In the end, it was the thought of killing her mother's grandchild that prevented her from having an abortion. Her little boy is now two years old, and she is happy with her decision. She believes that she wouldn't have been able to live well with herself if she had aborted her baby.

But, the young women said, that's why so many teenagers end up having babies they are unable to look after, because birthing the baby and keeping the baby in the family are the only options the teenagers believe are available to them. They said there is intense pressure to keep their children in their community and out of reach of the authorities. Even if their family did not have the financial and social resources to incorporate them into the household, the family would not let the baby be put up for adoption at birth. But the young women also said that, while many young parents have good intentions, they often can't keep up with the demands of raising the child, and many children

It's such a bad thing. That's just what we learn from our families and community in general. You just don't have abortions. So even the girls who have them don't talk about them. I only told my boyfriend and one other person who needed to drive me to the hospital. I could trust her. It was hard. How was I going to get to the hospital early in the morning without anyone asking any questions? It's a dark topic. It's not a good thing. I'd say abortion is worse than beating your wife. You can go ahead and beat your kids or give your kid to the grandparent. You can completely neglect your kids, but if you have an abortion, oh my god, that's murder.

I think it scars emotionally when girls have abortions. We feel the shame. The whole thing about life is so scary. Then down the road, like, I'm thinking I could have had a baby. The shame and guilt sticks right out.

I didn't really have any teachings about abortion, but there is a lot of criticism in the community about women who have them so you know what people think. When I was young my mom said you made your bed, now lie in it. I made my decision. I missed my shot. I decided to have my baby. If it was impossible for me to raise my child I may have made a different decision. But if I had had an abortion, I would have had guilt for the rest of my life because I could have looked after that child if I had tried.

are later lost to the foster care system. Most extended families step in and try to keep the children within the family, but they may be too overextended already to succeed.

All the young women in this conversation birthed their first baby and raised it in the family. Perhaps surprisingly, subsequent pregnancies were not often treated differently. Once the young women had one child, they knew what to expect. They realized that their goal of giving their child a good life was harder than they thought and wouldn't have wanted to make the situation even worse. Still, none of the young moms considered adoption for subsequent pregnancies. (At the time of writing, none of them had their children in the care of the system, although a few were constantly worried that the authorities could come at any time and take their children.)

A few of them did have abortions for subsequent pregnancies, although for each of those young women the abortion created a dissonance they had yet to resolve. As one young woman said, "I had a feeling I would be really upset after the abortion but I never imagined I would be as upset as I was. If I didn't have my other kid I would be a lot damn closer to suicide. The only thing that stopped me was my kid." Another young woman began self-mutilating after her abortion. She said, "You can't go back. No, I wouldn't go back. But you have done something wrong. Your community says it's wrong. You know it's wrong. And you aren't going to go to anyone for help because if you tell them they will tell the rest of the community, so what are you going to do?"

Strict moral teachings against abortion are, of course, not limited to First Nations. However, other cultures that forbid abortions also commonly have strong prohibitions regarding sexual activity for youths. At this time in First Nations culture, the young people are free to have sex, yet deeply conflicted about having abortions. It's not hard to understand why so many Aboriginal teenagers have babies they can't look after, or have abortions they can't live with.

My family doesn't want to give up children no matter what. We want to keep our children in the family. We don't let them go.

I was scared to tell my mom at first. When I did finally tell her I was already six months pregnant and there was nothing she could do. A lot of other people, my doctor and others, said give my child up for adoption and all this. I started freaking out and saying "Mom, we gotta get out of here." There were about five couples who wanted to adopt her. They were coming to my house. I never did know where the people were coming from. Finally my mom raised hell and told them to get the fuck out. My mom was really supportive when she decided we could do it ourselves. Maybe I was only thirteen and pregnant but she understood I was young and there was nothing she could do about that so she supported me to keep the baby.

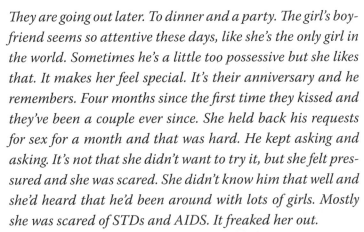

7

BEING PREGNANT

They are going out later. To dinner and a party. The girl's boy-friend seems so attentive these days, like she's the only girl in the world. Sometimes he's a little too possessive but she likes that. It makes her feel special. It's their anniversary and he remembers. Four months since the first time they kissed and they've been a couple ever since. She held back his requests for sex for a month and that was hard. He kept asking and asking. It's not that she didn't want to try it, but she felt pressured and she was scared. She didn't know him that well and she'd heard that he'd been around with lots of girls. Mostly she was scared of STDs and AIDS. It freaked her out.

Since they did it, they've been inseparable. She is excited about their night but she's scared. This time she's not afraid of diseases; she's sure they'll be together forever. She's afraid she's pregnant. She has missed her last two periods. Missing one was bad enough but she waited and waited again last week and nothing.

She tells her mom she is meeting her friends in the village but instead she catches the bus and goes to the walk-in medical clinic. The doctor helps her with a pregnancy test.

84

The fluid is supposed to change colour and hers turns as blue as the sky. It feels like her knees are filling up with water. She leans against the clinic bed while her body swims in the air.

"We'll do another test in the lab," the doctor says. "But I don't think there's any mistake. You are pregnant."

She is quiet through dinner. Her boyfriend is disappointed, she can tell. He wants her to be excited about tonight. "Come on," he says. "What's up with you? You on your rag?"

She wishes she were.

"We got four cases of beer and a bottle of rye." She knows that is meant for her, too. They had planned to get wasted. The party is at her cousin's place so she doesn't even have to make it home tonight.

She decides right then to forget the bad news she had from the doctor. Her boyfriend is getting angry with her and she is going to spoil the whole evening if she doesn't change her attitude.

"Yeah, it's going to be great," she says. Then she laughs a lot. Even more than usual.

Later she drinks a lot more than usual as well. It works. Her boyfriend is all over her and she gets completely wasted. She wakes up on top of him in the morning, but she can't remember much of the night other than she knows they were together.

She pukes in the morning, pukes and pukes. It is the worst hangover she has ever had. She tells everyone she has the flu. Now she is really scared. She knows drinking is no good for the baby. She has heard something about fetal alcohol syndrome, where the baby doesn't get the right stuff to grow or the alcohol gets in the way of the brain or something. But she knows if she stops drinking, especially with her boyfriend, then everyone will know she's pregnant.

She drinks the next weekend and the weekend after that. She totally drinks, more than she has ever drunk in her life.

She feels good while she is drinking. She forgets about how scared she was. And another thing; she has heard that sometimes drinking makes the fetus come early. Maybe she will have a miscarriage and then she won't be pregnant anymore. When she really thinks about that she freaks right out, but something inside secretly hopes it will happen. When she gets drunk that secret feeling makes her drink more and more.

The baby doesn't come. She doesn't want it to. She starts thinking about the baby. She imagines it moving around inside although she can't really feel anything for sure. Her boyfriend loves kids, she knows that, because he always plays on the floor with his little cousins. Now she is more scared to tell him because he'll be mad that she has drunk so much. Everyone will be mad. But her tummy has started to get big and she has no choice but to tell. At least it will stop her from acting so crazy.

Even though most of the young women were pretty sure that they were pregnant before they got their test results, the words from the doctor still came as a shock. For some of them, getting their tongue around the words "I am pregnant" was even harder. Typically, they spent the first few days after receiving the news in a state of semi-denial. While their condition consumed their attention, it was still easier to pretend it didn't exist.

Each young woman had her own reasons for not wanting to face up to her pregnancy. Some were afraid to disappoint their families, others were scared that their boyfriends might get angry, and others worried about school and teachers or friends. More often than not, the young women were deeply disappointed in themselves, and needed time to get used to the idea of being pregnant. They also felt a sense of unfairness—that they were simply the unlucky ones.

"Now when people look at me, they only think one thing," one young woman said. "They think: that girl's had sex. It's so unfair. It's not like only the pregnant girls have had sex. Think about it."

They had various strategies to break the news to people. Most of them told their boyfriend first, and a few told their mother or a girlfriend before they told anyone else. "Then," as one young woman said, "you wait and freak out trying to avoid everyone until you are sure they all know. Then you sort of take a deep breath and face up to them." In any case, it wouldn't have taken long for the news to spread. No news travels faster in First Nations communities than "You'll never guess who's pregnant"—especially if the young woman is only fourteen or fifteen years old.

Two of the young women had actually wanted to be pregnant. But even they were surprised to find that they had feelings of shame, embarrassment, guilt, and disappointment when they told their families.

The young women said they thought that the high level of tolerance in First Nations com-

My boyfriend and me went to the doctor's office and got the test. The doctor called us in and said: "The test is positive." I looked at my boyfriend and thought, what does positive mean? What does a positive test mean? Does that mean it's good? He was looking just as confused as me. Then the doctor kept talking and I realized that it meant I was pregnant. My head was swimming. It was so weird.

I don't know what we are so afraid of. It's not like anyone is going to hit you or anything. It's more the disappointment. It's more about your own disappointment with yourself.

I felt like I let my family down. I was going to be the first of all my grandparents' grandchildren to graduate. She's going to be our lawyer. I'm, like, I can still be a lawyer. I can still go back to school. But now people look at me and think that all I'm going to do with my life is have babies. They don't see me like their lawyer anymore.

I was so guilty. I was going to graduate and I wanted to finish high school. I was sure Mom was going to find out. It was, like, okay, I gotta tell her. She said, "It's okay." I was, like, "Mom, I don't want you to be mad." She said, "I'm happy as long as you are happy."

munities makes it easier for First Nations teenagers to come to terms with a pregnancy. Still, all the young women, whether they came from a disrupted and unsupportive family or not, had believed they would be the ones in their families to successfully complete high school. They had all wanted to avoid becoming another pregnant Indian girl. They'd wanted to prove to themselves and others that they could walk the First Nations teenage gauntlet and get to the age of twenty without getting pregnant. The benign resignation that they faced from their families and friends—there you go, just another statistic, what do you expect—was almost harder to face than blatant shock, and, in a way, far more debilitating. The sad reality was that everyone, including themselves, was prepared for them to fail. That was the worst feeling of all.

Family response varied slightly, but in the end the young women's stories were similar. Following a brief period of surprise and disappointment, without exception all their families responded with unqualified acceptance. The families of their boyfriends had the same response to the news of a baby. In fact, more than half of the young women lived with the baby's father's family immediately after giving birth, and were supported by the paternal grandmother.

Such ready acceptance of teenage pregnancies in Aboriginal communities could be seen as consistent with traditional First Nations respect for life and inclusion of children into the family and community. Many front-line workers, however, believe that the reaction is far less positive in its implications. They say that because there are so many pregnant teenagers there is little social pressure to avoid pregnancy, thereby encouraging a sense of complacency.

One grandmother said, "Young people don't get married first.

They hardly even date. The way we are doing things is completely out of order. Young people get together and a few months later we find out she's pregnant, even if she's just a little girl and he's still a little kid. These young men don't want to settle down and be fathers. They aren't thinking about making a family. Neither one of them know how to be parents. They just kind of fall into a relationship and end up with kids. And now we're getting used to it—the family and community I mean. It's common now. Parents and grandparents let the kids shack up in the basement like it's an okay thing to do. The truth is: this is really getting out of control."

The problem is compounded by the fact that these pregnancies are not arising out of long-term, mature, and committed relationships. Out of the thirteen young women, only one of them had been with her boyfriend for more than a year when she became pregnant. None of the others had chosen their boyfriends to be their life partners (in part a reflection of their age). Their relationship simply became defined by the pregnancy.

Very few of the young women had a satisfying relationship with the fathers of their babies. Any love and compatibility in their relationships were replaced by logistics, shared experience, and mutual need as the basis for the partnership.

For the young fathers-to-be, a feeling of being cornered evoked

My mom was disappointed because, like, when I was younger she was really strict with me. I wasn't able to do anything and then she didn't like my boyfriend. We drank and partied. But now it's okay. She said she was proud of me. I think getting pregnant made us closer. It made me feel better once she said that to me. She said she was happy. Now having a baby, she's always phoning me.

I was really scared to tell my mom that I was pregnant. But when it came time to tell her it was fine. She was young as well when she had me. She probably understood. My grandparents were just regular grandparents, all lovey-dovey about it.

a number of unsurprising responses. When they first heard their girlfriend was pregnant, whether or not they loved her, some of them wanted to run away. That response was usually overcome by a grudging acceptance of responsibility. One young man was excited and afraid, but ready to care for his child no matter what. Overall, however, having a baby was the farthest thing from their minds, and they were less prepared and less willing to stick it out than the young women. They just wanted to keep on partying. Most of the relationships didn't last long.

It was different, of course, for the young women. What was the point of wishing you could run away? One young woman actually broke up with her boyfriend when she realized she was pregnant, because she did not want to have a committed relationship with him. But she was the exception. For the others, once they were pregnant they clung to their boyfriends whether they had intended to stay with the young men or not. Some of them simply wanted a father for their baby. Others really believed that they could create a family that would stay together. Some just didn't think any other boy would want a girlfriend or wife who already had a baby, so they hung on to the one they had tenaciously.

But hanging on came at a high emotional cost. They were afraid that if they didn't give the boy everything he wanted and needed—including, of course, sex—then he would simply find another girl who would. That was guaranteed to make otherwise confident young women jealous and insecure. As their pregnancies developed, their fears increased along with their girth. One young woman who gained almost 45 kilograms watched helplessly as her boyfriend started flirting with other girls. Another young woman felt nauseated for the first four or five months of her pregnancy, and having sex was the farthest thing from her mind. Pregnancy didn't have the same effect on her boyfriend, of course. The demands upon her when she was not feeling well were hard to take. Once she started to look pregnant, however, he stopped wanting to have sex with her and started looking around at other girls. That was even worse.

She tried to satisfy him, but he said he didn't find pregnant girls attractive.

Some of the young women experienced quite a different reaction from their boyfriends, although no less disturbing and certainly not emotionally supportive in its implications. The young men in question saw pregnancy as a mark of ownership, as if they had publicly registered a permanent claim: "She's pregnant, and she's mine." One young woman's boyfriend told her after she became pregnant that no one else would want her. In that case, he didn't have to worry about losing her anymore. He had put into words what many of the young women feared—no one else would want them in their condition. As a result they hung on to unstable and sometimes abusive relationships because they thought that they had nowhere else to go.

Of course there were exceptions, and at least one young woman was lucky enough to have a boyfriend who was patient and "pretty understanding" about sex. "He knew it was hard for me when I was pregnant and even worse once baby was born. He's gentle with me. I don't think he likes it but what can he do?"

Becoming pregnant as a teenager changes every relationship that the teenager has. One moment she's her

I just didn't want anything to do with sex. After I got pregnant the last thing I wanted was sex. That's all he wanted.

He thought I was being cold and that I didn't want him anymore. It was like he took it personally. What was I supposed to do with that? I didn't know how to deal with his feelings.

I think he wanted me pregnant so that other guys wouldn't look at me. He got less jealous when I was pregnant. He said no one else would want me now. But then he's still looking around out there. I know he is.

I lived with my boyfriend and his father and they treated me like a princess. Anything I wanted they got for me especially when I was pregnant. They cooked for me. I didn't do much of anything.

I guess everybody expected more from me. Back when I wasn't pregnant I was Daddy's little girl. Every time I saw him he would give me forty bucks. I would go to the movies. He would be there for me. When he found out I was pregnant it stopped. He expected more from me.

family's little girl, or rebellious teenager, or perfect daughter, and the next moment she is something entirely different. Pregnant teenagers exist in limbo: not adult, not typical teenager, not mother, no longer child—and it's hard for them and for their families to make sense of that. Relationships can be permanently destroyed. They are always changed.

One young woman's father responded to the news of her pregnancy with a gruff, "Well, now you are pregnant, it's obvious that you have made an adult decision, so it's time to act like an adult." She wanted to cry, "Daddy, I'm still your little girl." She was only fifteen, and not ready to be an adult. But her relationship with her father changed forever. He never called her his little girl anymore, or gave her money on Fridays so she could go to a movie with her friends. He didn't take her shopping for clothes or to his baseball games. Her parents did become friends with her boyfriend, and allowed him to stay with her. But her father also started drinking on weekends with her boyfriend, while she stayed home. To her it felt as if her boyfriend had become more like part of the family than she was. All the same, he left her when she was eight months pregnant. Suddenly, she had no boyfriend, and no family that resembled the one she had previously known.

One young woman had a completely different experience. When she was younger, she had been "Mommy's girl." Most of her time was spent with her mother and grandmother, at least until a few months before she became pregnant. At that time, she was sixteen and had begun to feel suffocated by her family's involvement in her life. For the first time she was stepping out to be with her friends. Her parents didn't like her new attitude or her new boyfriend, and

tried to keep her home. But she rebelled against their control. Within months of starting to date her boyfriend, she became pregnant. When her boyfriend continued to party, she found herself back at home on Friday nights with Mom and Grandma: exactly what she had been trying to avoid. However, this time it was completely different. To her surprise, she was being treated as an adult, and with more respect. When she realized that, the bitterness she felt about her situation was softened.

A few young women, especially those who were not close to their families, actually enjoyed the recognition and attention they started to receive from aunts and grandmothers. It wasn't until she became pregnant that one young woman got to know her grandmother. Suddenly, her grandmother began to treat her as if overnight she had passed from childhood to adulthood, and began talking to her about family matters and community concerns. This was not necessarily easy to adjust to, however, especially for a teenager who still felt like a child and wasn't at all ready to fit into her new, supposedly adult role. But having become pregnant, she had no choice. In one way or another, pregnancy thrust all the young women into the world of adults without any preparation.

Elders and front-line workers told us about some of the traditional coming-of-age rituals and practices that once marked the transition from childhood to adulthood, and the changing roles that young people would experience in a Coast Salish family and community. Each family had its own way of practising the coming-of-age traditions, but they had much in common. At the onset of a girl's first period, she would be taken into the care of an older woman. Usually, the girl was off limits to everyone except her mentor, who taught her the roles and responsibilities of a woman, mother, and mature family and community member.

The coming-of-age ritual symbolically led the girl out of the world of being cared for by others, and into the world of caring for others. From daybreak to sunset, the girl's hands were never idle. She cooked, cleaned, knitted, wove, and did whatever else was considered women's work. During her three or four days of isolation, she learned the meaning of being a woman in Coast Salish society. She also came to know the mystery of her body that now could reproduce life. A public ceremony often followed the girl's seclusion, to acknowledge her new maturity as well as the community's responsibility to respect and protect her.

One family used what was called a "swing ceremony" to mark a girl's transition to womanhood. When he was a boy, said the elder who described it, there was a swing hanging from a giant maple tree near the beach where he lived. When a girl began to menstruate, she was placed on the swing with a rope tied at one end around her waist and held at the other by one of her grandmothers. All the female members of her family circled the swing chanting words that meant "girl" and "woman." Back and forth she would swing, until at one of the repetitions of "woman," the grandmother would pull the girl from the swing and cut the rope, thus signifying the severance of the umbilical cord and the end of the girl's childhood.

Coming-of-age rituals existed for boys, as well, signalled by the changes occurring in their voices. A mentor took the boy into the bush to learn outdoor survival skills and his responsibilities as a Coast Salish man, future husband, and future father.

Most of the young women in our project had heard about coming-of-age ceremonies, although only one had taken part in a ritual when she first menstruated. A few grandmothers we talked to suggested that the coming-of-age ceremonies could be adapted to recognize the changes that come with pregnancy instead of menstruation. Mentors could teach the mother- and father-to-be the skills and knowledge they will need, and show them their rightful place in the community.

In tandem with such mentoring, cultural prohibitions such as the following could perhaps be put into their proper context: Don't eat strawberries if you are pregnant, or your baby will have a red blotch on its body. Don't pet puppies or kittens, or your baby will be covered in hair. Don't eat crabs, or your baby will walk with bowed

I don't think I really believe all those teachings. But my cousin ate a lot of strawberries and her baby had a big strawberry mark on her neck so I didn't eat any—just to be sure.

I was dying for some crabs after baby was born. My grandma says that if you eat crabs the baby will walk sideways. Even then baby had bowed legs.

It's not me, it's my boyfriend who believes all those stories about what to do and what not to do when you're pregnant. His mother really believes it, too, so when I was pregnant I wasn't allowed to pet animals, eat crabs, use knitting needles, eat strawberries—that was the worse part because it was right in strawberry season and I love strawberries.

legs. "Young people know these teachings," said one grandmother. "But there are so many other traditional practices and teachings relating to pregnancy that they know nothing about."

The young women didn't know where the taboos had originated, or whether there was any reason to believe that they remained relevant. But only a handful of the young women questioned them. Some were outwardly dismissive of them as just "old wives' tales," but most of the young women were unwilling to risk the possible consequences that could result from ignoring the warnings. There was a strong "it's better to be safe than sorry" attitude among them, and the young men had a similar attitude.

Smoking and drinking while pregnant are becoming the new taboos: *If you smoke when you're pregnant, your baby could get asthma. If you drink, especially in the first few months of pregnancy, the baby won't be able to learn properly, or it could be born with weird teeth.* Some of the young women stopped smoking and drinking the moment they knew they were pregnant. But most of them were still far more likely to restrict their intake of strawberries and crabs than alcohol and cigarettes. Perhaps the traditional status of the strawberry taboo gave it extra weight in their minds than mainstream information about smoking and drinking while pregnant, which was received with more skepticism or apathy.

Most of their families were not talking about the negative effects of smoking and drinking while pregnant, despite the fact that members of those families had fetal alcohol syndrome (FAS) or fetal alcohol effects (FAE). Only a few of the older young mothers had heard a medical explanation of FAS, and none of them clearly understood the real implications for the baby of smoking and drinking while they were pregnant.

A youth culture heavily mired in drinking and drugs is a trap for teenagers who become pregnant. They are faced with a difficult conundrum. Drinking, especially when you are first pregnant, can be a social imperative. If a young woman stops drinking suddenly, she is effectively making a public statement that means only one thing—she must be pregnant—not a fact she is necessarily ready to admit to everyone. So until they can no longer hide their condition, teenage moms are at an enormous risk of succumbing to that damaging behaviour.

There are ways to get around that. One young woman was fifteen and had started dating her boyfriend

As soon as I found out I was pregnant I stopped drinking. There's no way I was going to take a chance on that. I tell everyone to stop when I see them drinking. You should stop smoking as well.

All my friends were drinking and handing me drinks and giving me everything. I was six months pregnant and they still gave me drinks.

No one said anything to me to try and stop me. They gave me drinks. My friends, even some of my family. The only one that said anything to me was my boyfriend's mom. After she found out she told me that I shouldn't be drinking. She said, "I don't want my grandchild to have any problems." But even before she told me I felt terrible. But when I was thinking about it I was, like, I want to go out and drink and I don't want to think about it anymore. Then I did and afterwards it was, like, why did I do that?

Even my mom didn't tell me what really happens and why. She told me it's not that good for the baby but she didn't tell me what was really going on in my body. It's so scary now. It's hard to read the stuff about it. It's hard to think about.

I know a lot of girls who drink through their pregnancy. They should learn about it. I didn't know that much about fetal alcoholism. It's not that I didn't choose to know about it. I just wasn't right out there. I had heard about it but I didn't look right into it. After I got older I looked into it, and I was, like, oh, if everyone knew all that stuff about FAS they would think different. We aren't getting the message out there to the kids early enough to make them really aware of what it's about. It would have helped me to know about it earlier. I think they should have workshops in schools. They have workshops for moms but that's a bit late. They need the info before they get to be moms.

only a few months before she found out she was pregnant. They weren't a real couple yet, but she wasn't ready to lose him. She decided she should wait to break the news of her pregnancy until they had been together at least a few more months. But her boyfriend drank a lot, and drinking had become something she did every weekend—it was what they did together. She had heard about FAS and was worried that her baby was already affected because she had been drinking heavily for the previous two months.

Her dilemma was that she wanted to stop drinking immediately, but she thought her boyfriend would dump her as soon as he discovered the truth. She couldn't tell her friends, because they were into drinking as well. She couldn't tell her parents, because they would be angry—they didn't like either her boyfriend or her other friends. She was an emotional mess and she didn't know how to cope. She felt cornered and afraid. Her first strategy was to pretend that she had the flu, which worked for a few days. But when the weekend came around the only way to hide her pregnancy was to go out and party as usual. This time, she picked up a can of beer and carried it around, pretending to drink it. When no one was looking she headed to the bathroom or kitchen to pour the drink down the sink undetected, so she could be seen to be discarding her "empty" and starting another drink. She feigned drunkenness sufficiently well to convince her friends. She felt like a fraud, but she said faking it was better than living with the knowledge that she was harming her baby.

Many young women use smoking and drinking as tools to cope with their fears and frustrations about their pregnancy. That makes it doubly hard to quit. But many of those who continue to smoke and drink do so because they are not convinced that they are putting their baby at risk, or because they are simply so addicted that they need help to quit. FAS and the effects of smoking on the unborn child are not risks that are vivid enough in their minds to deter them from their actions. Indeed, some may even hope that the damaging effects of alcohol and smoke will terminate the pregnancy. As one young woman said, "Some girls just aren't ready for it. That's the thing about it. Native people are so strong against abortion so you can't have an abortion to get rid of your baby. Then they think maybe if they drink enough they will lose their baby. One woman drank for two or four days before she lost her baby. You can lose a baby that way."

Although health and community workers are spreading the

I didn't want to be pregnant so I kept doing what I was doing before. I kept drinking and it wasn't until I really acknowledged that I was pregnant that I knew I had to quit. It wasn't, like, every day or anything. But I kept going so no one would know I was pregnant. My cousins were around me and they drank. I knew it wasn't right and I knew it would hurt the baby. I was so scared all the time. But if I quit everyone would know I was pregnant and I didn't want anyone to know. I knew it was wrong to drink but I didn't know anything about it, really, not what was going on with my baby. I was just told, don't drink or something will happen.

I found out I was pregnant long before I told anyone. I was smoking and drinking. I couldn't stop. I smoked and drank for a while after I was pregnant. I was, like, oh God, I gotta go out. That's all I thought about. My doctor told me I had to stop. I don't know if that was it or what really made me stop, but I was drinking four or five days a week and I was smoking almost a pack of smokes a day. It was really bad.

It was so hard to stop. I knew I should. But I was so scared and uptight. When I tried to quit smoking I was having big headaches and I was twitching and everything. As soon as I would have a smoke I was better. So I had to deal with addiction and being pregnant. I like it better now I've quit. No smoking or drinking. I'm jogging and I'm healthy. Drinking was a lot harder to quit than smoking. I quit smoking after about four months. I was drinking pretty heavy when I quit. I wanted to stop.

word about the effects of smoking and drinking and drugs, there is still an enormous gap between what teenagers know and the harsh realities of FAS and FAE. There is a bigger gap yet between what they know and what they are prepared to act upon. As with the manner in which they became pregnant in the first place, the immediate concern or desire—in this case, concealing their condition, relieving their stress, or simply feeding an overwhelming addiction—takes priority over the long-term impacts of their actions. Because the effects do not necessarily show for years, it is easy for these young women to continue to deny that their substance use has had any effect on their child.

Their best hope may eventually be their own friends, if enough of the right information gets out to teenagers and more young people become convinced of the risks of drinking while pregnant. If the critical mass of thinking changes, friends may start to prevent pregnant friends from drinking or smoking. A few of the older young mothers said they believed this was beginning to happen. They said that at parties it is no longer uncommon to hear someone tell a pregnant girl to stop drinking

If I see a pregnant girl drinking now I'd tell her if I was her friend. I don't know if anything is wrong with my baby because I was drinking. I'll never know for sure. After I had my baby I started to see commercials and things written about drinking and smoking mothers. I never saw it before or I never took it seriously.

When a girl is pregnant the other girls try and take care of you even though they are young too. They are, like, get away from the smoke and get away from the drinking. It is way out of the question. If you are drinking when you are pregnant, people will be right against you even if they don't really know what is going on.

or to butt out her cigarette, but there is still the counterpressure to mind your own business.

Addiction remains a serious problem in the fight against FAS. Some young mothers have been drinking and smoking for years by the time they get pregnant. Young fathers are often in the same position, and are sometimes the reason a pregnant teenager won't quit or becomes critically addicted. Many young women get into drinking in the first place to keep up with their boyfriends. The targets for a preventive education campaign clearly should not be limited to young women at risk.

Simply managing personal health can be a struggle for pregnant teenagers, regardless of addiction or mere bad habits. The

One of my friends at school was pregnant and she was arguing with her boyfriend and she started drinking. I was, like, freaking out at her. And she was, like, well, what's it going to do. I was, like, I don't know that much about it, but I know it will hurt your baby. She stopped drinking after a few drinks and then we went upstairs and I asked my auntie and she said it could stop your baby from developing.

If someone is pregnant other girls will tell you to stop drinking. It's out there—girls know, but they don't know that much about it.

I was concerned about my weight so I stayed in sports. I took care of my body when I was pregnant. I put lotion on areas that would stretch and I don't have bad stretch marks. It is when I have problems with my boyfriend that I have problems with my eating habits.

young women knew they should eat a balanced diet, take vitamin supplements, have plenty of sleep, and exercise daily while they were pregnant. But even before they became pregnant, most of them had not acquired good eating and exercise habits. Most of them couldn't afford to eat the recommended diet for expectant mothers, nor did they have control over the food that was purchased in their homes, so they ate whatever was in the refrigerator. Only a few of them knew how to prepare their own meals properly, so they ended up eating "quick and easy" foods that often lacked real nutritional value. A snack often meant ice cream, and dinner out meant a trip to McDonald's.

As for sleep, it had less priority than whatever their friends were doing. The young women didn't have a place to exercise and they didn't have the time or money to go to the gym or to play sports. When they were getting close to full term, a few of them walked regularly to try to improve their chances for a good delivery. But for the most part only a few of them paid attention to their health. Only half of them visited a doctor or midwife regularly throughout their pregnancy.

The others visited only near the end of their pregnancy, and one young woman never saw a doctor until her delivery.

Predictably, given their lifestyles, most of them gained too much weight when they were pregnant. Anemia and lethargy plagued them throughout their pregnancies. While none of the young women in our project suffered additional health problems, gaining too much pregnancy weight puts women at higher risk of gestational diabetes, pre-eclampsia, and birth complications.

Three of the young women were different from the rest; they were vigilant about their health throughout their pregnancies. But their effort seemed to have less to do with their circumstances than with the young women's particular characteristics—they had always looked after themselves, and their bodies and health were priorities.

All the young women birthed their babies vaginally, two with birthing coaches rather than doctors. Most of them had their boyfriend, mother, and at least two or three other members of their families along with friends attending the birth. Most of their stories about giving birth were as much about discomfort, pain, and fear as they were about excitement and

My body went downhill when I was pregnant. After the fourth month of pregnancy I started gaining weight faster than I thought I would. By the ninth month, a few days before I had baby, I weighed close to 100 pounds more than I did before I got pregnant. Before I had her I didn't have all the tests you were supposed to have. One month before having my baby I went in and had blood work done only to find out my iron was three. I don't know what it's supposed to be but that was pretty low. I had to get shots to get my iron up. I also had high blood pressure and had to be on medication after baby was born. As soon as I had baby I dropped about 50 pounds but I'm still way bigger than I was before.

I walked thirty minutes a day until I had my baby. I know it made my delivery easier.

Once we got to the hospital my contractions were five minutes apart. They didn't hurt that much and when Mom and Grandma got there I was still walking up and down the hall. By the time son was born it was like my whole family and all my friends were there and they were all noisy and everything. The nurses kept telling people where to sit and stuff. Then everyone passed him around. I was, like, it's my turn.

Even when I'm depressed I try and do my hair and wash up and dress up. I have to for my son. So I keep going. I go to counselling and see the doctor but just because I have a baby now doesn't mean I'm going to give up. In fact I work harder now that he's born.

victory, although one young woman recalled, "I was the best patient. My doctor said I was so strong." Another young mom said she didn't know very much about the birthing process and was afraid when she finally went into labour, but when the pain came she just focused on what her doctor told her to do. When her baby finally arrived she said it hadn't been as bad as she had expected.

Mental health was not something the young women had thought about much, although most of them had experienced periods of feeling down in the dumps at some point during their pregnancy or early motherhood. Some of the young moms talked about how they cried all the time, or how they didn't want to get out of bed in the morning, as if it was something all young moms experienced—isn't that just the way it is when you are sixteen and have a one-year-old baby? Consequently only one young woman had been officially diagnosed as having postpartum depression. For the rest, if they were depressed, their conditions were left unidentified and untreated.

As one young mom said, "You just push your way through it until something clicks and then it gets easier. At least for a while."

8

We're Adults and Parents

 ◇◇◇

The girl's alarm clock sounds like a fire truck charging through an intersection.

It can't be six o'clock already, *she says to herself as she rolls over and shuts it off.* It feels like I only just went to sleep.

Then she peeks under the covers at her baby boy, who is fast asleep. From the peaceful look on his face it's hard to believe he was crying half the night in pain from his sprouting teeth.

"Okay, baby boy," she says out loud. "You can stay asleep until I'm ready to go and then I'm going to be the one who wakes you up."

The girl picks up her biology textbook and flips through the fifty pages she didn't have time to study the night before. She checks the headings and tries to remember how all the information fits together. She had promised herself and her teacher that she would study and get a good grade on the final exam. Biology is her favourite subject and she's good at it, too. If she's going to be a nurse she has to do well in anatomy. After ten minutes she puts her textbook into her knapsack and then stuffs in her study notes and exercise books.

A quick shower, a quick drink of juice, a quick choice of clothes, a quick comb through the hair and a ponytail; then into the diaper bag go milk, diapers (which reminds the girl that she has to go easy on how many she uses, there are only ten more and they have to last until the end of the week), cream for his bum and the stuff she got from the nurse for his gums, a jar of mixed fruit (that's all she can find so hopefully the daycare has some lunch for the kids—and he's going to need some eggs or something for breakfast), an extra two sets of clothes, and the girl is ready to wake up her baby.

"I'm so sorry, little boy," she says quietly as she kisses his nose. "I wish I could climb back in bed with you and then you could sleep as long as you want. But not today, buddy. Mommy has to write a test first thing this morning and you and me gotta get going."

A quick diaper change, a quick wash, a quick change of clothes; jackets, the stroller, the knapsack, the diaper bag, mittens because it's cold, and the girl and her baby head up the road. She has to hurry because it usually takes fifteen minutes to walk to school and she has left herself only twelve minutes.

When they arrive she drops him off in the daycare, tosses him a quick kiss, and heads to class. She flops into her desk and feels weirdly relieved even though the anatomy exam is facing her. At least now she can relax and breathe. Luckily she recognizes most of what she reads on the paper; luckily she can remember most of what she skimmed the night before and just before school. With a little more luck the girl figures she will at least get a passing grade—even if she didn't sleep the night before and even if she didn't get to study as she had promised herself.

◇◇◇

First Nations teen parents have incredibly complex lives. They get mixed messages from the media and their community about sexuality. They get contradictory messages and expectations in regard to having a family, getting an education, becoming employed, and partying. They have to deal with overcrowding and other aspects of poverty, as well as the clash of cultures. Young women in particular are expected to make the enormous transition from teenager to "instant" adult woman and mother.

Almost all of these young women inevitably are starting their adult lives as parents in poverty and disadvantage. In the face of what appear to be insurmountable obstacles, many of them are digging deeply into their internal resources of resilience, courage, and common sense, and becoming the women First Nations depend upon to rebuild their communities. Perhaps because of their fast leap into adulthood, it seems also to be the young mothers who are going back to school in record numbers, and who hold important positions in First Nations offices.

Still, it is extremely difficult for these young parents to provide a stable life for their children so that

I haven't had dreams for years. I haven't wished for anything since I was about fourteen. I have a few people in my family that want to support me, but most of them don't really get around to it. So, instead of dreams, I have my own plans. I know what I want to do. I don't, like, stick to thinking about it all the time. So far in my life none of them have happened. That's why it's easier when I don't tell anyone.

I can't really say what happened to my dreams. The only thing I dreamed of when I was small was to get out of my mom's house and that happened as soon as I got pregnant when I was fourteen. Then my dream was to keep my own little family together. That was a shitty ride. After nine years and three children my dreams sort of crumbled. But I'm getting back on track now. I know where I want to go and I'm going to get there. School first and then I'll find a career.

I remember my mom and dad fighting and then I remember my mom and my brother's dad. Me and my brothers and sisters would go sit in the closet while my mom got beat up. Those aren't the kind of memories I want my son to have. When his dad and I started fighting I knew I had to leave. But now I'm not really sure if where I'm going will be that good for him. In the next couple of years I need to go to school. I want to set an example for him. . . . I want him to go further than me or my mom and dad or my grandparents.

the next generation doesn't have to repeat the cycle of poverty. There is no avoiding the simple fact that teenage parents lack proper parenting skills, even if they do manage to finish their education, get jobs, and become financially independent. These young people are expected to become instant adults—indeed, they have to—without, in most cases, any satisfactory societal framework to support them.

One young mother began to feel like a woman after her baby was born, but she didn't have any idea what it meant to be a woman. None of these young women had had the benefit of traditional Coast Salish mentoring (as described in the last chapter), and only a few had strong role models in their lives. Only three or four of them could immediately name a woman they looked up to as being the kind of woman and mother they would like to emulate. In general they also didn't know very many families that they considered strong and healthy. Nor did the young women or men see their reserve as a healthy place to live, let alone to raise their children. At the same time, they also loved their communities and wanted more than anything to live on the reserve, make it a good place, and have a good family.

The young women believe that their generation must become the best parents they can be and raise educated, disciplined, nonviolent children who can take advantage of all the good things the world has to offer. However, they know they need help. When asked what sorts of help they needed, they responded with suggestions including reading programs for children and their parents, sports and cultural activities for the children so that they can develop to their full potential, programs to reduce violence and use of drugs and alcohol in their communities so that the children will be safe, and education to encourage the children to take advantage of programs and lessons off the reserve.

But first and foremost, the young mothers wanted help to learn how to be an adult parent. One young mother from a neighbouring First Nation described her frustration with not being able to find the direction she needed within her community. "My counsellor told me, look inside yourself. You'll find the answers there. Or

We were allowed to watch violent movies and TV shows. My parents bought us guns and violent toys. I don't want my son to learn violence. I already don't let him watch it on TV and I don't buy him those kinds of toys. We were out of control when we were little. Everyone says no one would look after us. It's because no one taught us anything. I am going to teach my son to behave and not to be violent.

ask your family," she said. " I told her to forget it. What am I going to find there? My mother was an alcoholic and so was my grandmother. So my little boy is FAS. For that matter I'm probably FAS, too. I don't know how to be a mother. My mother didn't know how to be a mother, either. Where am I going to learn anything? I watch the women and mothers around me and that's how I figure out what *not* to do. I try and do the opposite. But it's a hard way to figure things out. I wish I had someone who would give me suggestions and advice. I need all the advice I can get." This young woman's comments reflected a repeating theme in our discussions. Most of the young women found that, in the absence of good role models, their ideas about how they wanted to live and raise their children became simply the opposite of what they saw around them.

Good partner and father role models were lacking for the young men as well. The young men wanted their children to have a good

I refuse to raise my children the way my mom raised me and my brothers and sisters. I will do everything to make sure that doesn't happen.

I wasn't raised by my parents very much. I was watched by whoever was around. It led me to be independent. I am able to get a clear picture myself of what I want to do with my child. I look at people in my family and I am raising my child the exact opposite of them.

I feel good that I am able to do it on my own. I may have broken a lot of cycles in my family. I found other ways of doing things. Like when I was younger, I would get a slap across the face or the butt and then be told if I wanted to cry I would get more. Or I would get thrown in a cold shower.

My daughter expects to get talked to, not hit, when she's in trouble, because that's what I do. I sit her down and talk to her and let her know there are other ways to handle her problems. When I was a child I was yelled at or hit. When I see that in a house I get that feeling of not being understood as a child. It makes me feel mad and frustrated and mostly it makes me feel scared.

father, but most of them just didn't know how to pull that off. Neither did the young women. They all thought of a good father as one who spent time with the mother and child(ren), helped out around the house, and provided financially. But for the young men, their chief experience in life was playing sports and "hanging out." Few of them had the skills to create a family structure that balanced work, entertainment, and family responsibilities, let alone to manage his own feelings and to provide proper emotional support to a young pregnant woman or new mother.

One young man's father and grandfather taught him about relationships and told him to treat his girlfriend the way he would his mother. They didn't say much about sexuality, and nothing about birth control. The rest of the young men learned the hard way, meaning they figured out how to be a father on their own. "You do what you watch," one young man said.

"And that means you are a role model to your kid even if you don't want to be." He said he once watched his three-year-old play out a fist fight he had witnessed. That's when he realized his behaviour was on display and had a big influence on his son. "I already regret a lot of things that I've done," he said. "But now I'm more careful."

One young man talked to his close family when he needed advice. The rest of them had no one to confide in. Once in a while they talked to their friends. But their friends didn't know much more about fathering than they did. And if there were few programs available for mothers, there were none at all for the young fathers.

The adult presences around these young couples can be more hindrance than help, and occasionally downright destructive. All young mothers want to create a nest for their baby: a safe, comfortable home. But obtaining proper housing was one of the biggest obstacles for the young mothers in their effort to create a stable family unit.

Multiple families living in one house is nothing new for First Nations, of course. Traditionally, Coast Salish people lived in large dwellings that housed entire extended families. That sense of extended family is still a strong concept today. What is new is the degree of overcrowding. It's common in today's First Nations communities for two or three families to live in one home, even if that home was built to house three or four people at most.

When most of the young women arrived home with their baby, they became part of a large group living in the same house, a group that might have included the baby's grandmother and grandfather, uncles, aunts, cousins, and more distant relatives. This might seem ideal in terms of plentiful family support, presumably allowing ample opportunity for the guidance and mentoring they all said they wanted. Unfortunately, in most cases, it meant that the young women had no control over their surroundings, and in some cases no control over how the baby was treated. The role of independent adult becomes blurry in these circumstances. It can be abdicated; it can also be taken away.

I didn't want to feed my baby sugar. I was so afraid he would get rotten teeth. Then one day when he was crying his auntie was feeding him a popsicle. I had a fit on her but she said he liked it. Then she made fun of me, saying stuff like "Poor baby, his mom won't even give him a popsicle." Pretty soon everyone is giving him popsicles because she's telling them all that he likes them. I hate it.

The needs of the baby and the young mother do not necessarily take precedence over the needs of the other people in the home. Some of the young women wanted their homes to be smoke-free, yet only a few were able to achieve their goal. If people smoked in the house before the baby was born, they continued to smoke there after it came home.

Love may be abundant; but the young mothers said they wanted their babies to get to bed at a decent time and they wanted them to be fed certain food, and it was hard for them to stay in control of their little family when there were so many other people in the house. If the baby whimpered, someone picked it up, or demanded that the mother pick it up, whether she wanted to or not. Most of the young women said that pretty soon they were carrying their babies around with them most of the day and sleeping with them at night, even though they would have preferred to leave them to sleep by themselves.

Motherhood, at any age, is a process of trial and error. Letting your baby cry or not cry, bathing in the morning or at night, supplementing with a bottle or only breastfeeding: these decisions and countless others are among the important choices a new mother needs to make. Some will work and some won't, but they all eventually help a mother decide what is right for her and her baby, and define her mothering style. All the young women started out with good intentions, but without the luxury of having space to themselves, the young couples had little opportunity to learn how to be parents in their own way.

By the time their children were one or two years old, and had been exposed to such a diversity of disciplinary measures all their short lives, they were unruly and presented control problems that were much too complicated for their young parents to handle.

Rules the young women set for their babies were often ignored by the extended family. One young woman found that, whatever she did, her boyfriend's mother would tell her she was wrong. His sisters would snatch her son out of her arms. She wanted a chance to do it on her own and learn from her mistakes, but it wasn't until her son was three years old that she was able to move out on her own. By then, he wouldn't listen to her, and his behaviour was out of control.

While the young women were determined to raise their children to know that they were loved, they were young and inexperienced with maintaining discipline. Most of them were afraid to establish boundaries. Elders say that traditional Coast Salish child-rearing methods did not include orthodox forms of punishment. Hitting, raised voices, calling for "time out," and reprimands were unknown, and children were free to explore and behave as they saw fit. They were part of a structured, viable, working family and community, and learned from

It's a struggle . . . every day. Each day I think about what it is I want to teach my daughter. I debate whether I am doing the right thing, or whether I should just raise her the way I was raised. I question my slack discipline skills and wonder whether she will eventually be worse off than I was because of that. Honestly, I don't know how to be a mother 100 percent of the time. I have lived with my own mother, my grandmother, a couple of aunts. Each of them plays a role in how I raise my daughter. I take skills, attitudes, beliefs, and teachings from each. As she gets older I question myself more and more. Lately I have heard things come out of my mouth that I once heard and hated my mother saying. That worries me. I don't want to be the kind of mother my mother was. I try. But how do you teach something you don't know?

I see kids around that rule their parents. I don't like what they look like. They're just little brats. I don't want my baby to turn out like that, but I don't think I'll know what to do about it either.

Discipline is the worst part. I can't say no without feeling guilty and then I change my mind. I want to discipline my son. I don't want him to get control of me but I can already feel it coming. I think it would be easier if he was a girl. He is so strong-minded that it's like he wins over me every time.

That's the part we need help with. How do you say no without being too hard on your kid? I sure don't know the answer to that one.

their play what their role in the family was to be and how to live up to expectations. In their contemporary world, however, most of the young women didn't have a family or community structure that set boundaries or determined expectations.

Today, if parents never say no, the child is faced with unlimited access to things like junk food and television, leading to behaviour problems. "It's so much harder now," one young woman noted. "There is so much kids can get into. The movies are so violent—everything he wants to watch is violent. It gets worse all the time. There's so much junk food out there. I'm just scared that when my son gets a little older he'll be doing stuff that really hurts him, like drugs and stuff. Then how am I going to say no to him?"

It is unclear whether their approach has more to do with honouring traditional Coast Salish child-rearing methods, or with simply still being teenagers; both are likely. All of the young women were unable to say no to their children without feeling guilty themselves, and all of them wanted to know how to get their children to behave and show respect, without being too hard on them.

Any discipline that did occur appeared to be a learned behaviour. The young women who were disciplined by their parents as children were the ones who seemed to have an easier time saying no

when they thought it was necessary. The young mothers who had been free to do what they pleased, however, and therefore had no model to follow, also had no practical tools to use to control their children. For those young women, administering discipline was like trying to speak a foreign language.

Guilt can be overpowering for teenage mothers. They are faced with an overwhelming sense of inadequacy, compounded by a perceived collective expectation that they will not do a good job. They are all too familiar with the stereotype into which they fall, and fear that it is true: that their children will suffer because they were raised by teenagers. The young women here wanted to prove to themselves and others that they could do a good a job of mothering, even though they often didn't believe they had the skills or resources for the job.

They were further inhibited by their community surroundings. Drugs, alcohol, violence, and infighting made the reserve a less than safe place to raise their babies. But family, culture, friends, and community made it difficult to think of living anywhere else. The reserve was the only home most of the young women had known. But if only there wasn't so much drinking and drugs, they kept saying. If only there wasn't so much violence. If only the people were not so angry, and didn't fight with each other so much. If only the reserve community was more accepting of outsiders. Then, they said emphatically, the reserves would be the greatest places in the world

I used to say I'm not going to discipline my son but he already needs it. He knows the word no.

You hear so much about the kids of teenage moms. It's all over the TV and people even tell you. It's like teenage moms are to blame for all the bad kids. Supposedly kids who had teenage moms get lower grades at school, have behaviour problems, get sick more often, have worse teeth; you name it, they got it. Then in the end they are going to end up criminals. What do you do with that? It makes you feel pretty guilty.

in which to live.

One young woman didn't want her son to think the boundaries around the reserve were the end of his world. If he was going to have the best life he could have, he would have to be able to live in both the Aboriginal and non-Aboriginal worlds. Another young woman had always thought of the world as divided into two: the reserve for First Nations people, and the rest of the world for everyone else. She noted that the reserve has many positive aspects to it, such as a strong sense of community, family, and culture, and she wanted her children to benefit from those aspects. But the reserve doesn't offer the same opportunities as the off-reserve world.

Like many First Nations young people she knew, this young woman rarely socialized off the reserve. She wanted her children to learn to swim or dance or take music lessons, but she found herself signing her children up only for activities that took place on the reserve. She was afraid to be the only First Nations parent at a school group or children's group, and she worried about how her children would feel

It was hard for me when my oldest started school. I would go and stand at the bus stop with the other parents. I was so young. I would try and hide away from them. When I got home I cried. "Look at me," I said. "Look at me. I'm just a kid and I'm pregnant again and there are all those parents there. They are all chit-chatting and I don't have anything to say. I can't even talk to people." I had to learn and after a while I'd talk to people and they weren't bad at all. I'm not so scared anymore. I don't think other people know how to act towards you. Sometimes now people will compliment us when we are out with our kids. They are amazed at how young we are and how the kids act.

when they were the only First Nations kids present. She believed her lack of experience and confidence to enter the off-reserve world had thwarted her chances at many opportunities, and now it was hindering her children's opportunities.

One grandmother said she can see her own children repeating

I was in grade eight when I got with my children's father. I liked going to school, but when I got with him I started to skip out. By the time I was in grade nine it was a different story. There was a smoking area and there were people selling drugs. I found a whole different crowd of people—the kind of people my boyfriend hung around. I had a smoke here and a smoke there, then I tried this drug and that drug and I got hooked on LSD so I quit going to class altogether. Two months into grade nine and I was pregnant.

I did some home-schooling but quit when my baby was born. I tried to go back to school after my second but didn't stick to it, and again after my third. I am now back at school, and sticking to it.

behaviour she exhibited when they were young—such as sending the children into school on their own because she was too afraid to go inside, haunted by bad memories of her school days. One young woman couldn't even take her child to the school bus on a daily basis because she couldn't face all the white mothers waiting with their children.

Unfortunately, many First Nations parenting programs focus on parenting from the prenatal to toddler stage, and end once a mother turns twenty. Community services for parents of young children, pre-adolescents, and teenagers are almost non-existent. But mothers who had babies when they were fourteen have preteen children when they are twenty-four, and again find themselves playing catch-up. They are parenting teenagers when they are barely out of their own teens, and they have next to no resources to draw upon. In terms of education, they are barely catching up with their peers; some may not be far ahead of their own children.

Continuing their own education was something the young women believed they could do something about. They had goals and believed that they would, eventually, achieve them. Education, in fact, stood out as an area that they could be proactive about, rather than simply let go with the passivity that coloured so much else about their lives.

For almost two decades, adult education has been a normal part of First Nations life and culture. Educational opportunities are promoted, daycares and subsidies are offered, and many are taking advantage of it, with optimism that they will succeed. Perhaps most importantly for these young women, they finally had role models. Most of them knew many women who had returned to school and graduated, or continued on in college and university.

The young women were frustrated but not defeated by the delay their baby caused in their plans. Education and career were still foremost in their plans; now it would just take longer. As one young woman said, "My education goals are the same; I just have to put them to the side for a little while. It's just a delay."

Unfortunately, structure was often lacking and it became hard for the young parents to deal with the demanding pace of modern culture. This was particularly a problem when they delayed entering the job market until they were in their mid-twenties. By the time they began working, especially the young dads, they felt too old for entry-level jobs, and they couldn't compete for jobs that required experience.

Keeping up with the demands of modern society is difficult for young people raised on "Indian time." It's not just another stereotype, and it's not just about arriving late to meetings. Life on the reserve is not often dictated by the stroke of the hour or marked by a linear stream of events. No one panics if the order of things is

When I was young I was positive I was headed straight for a good university. But after having a baby at a young age I had to put high school graduation on hold for a couple of years. Now I know again that my education will be a reality. I may not be able to do what I originally planned. I wanted to be a lawyer but with the time and energy it takes, maybe not. The stresses of being a single parent means I might go into being a teacher. I am slightly trapped now in Victoria and that limits what university I go to. I have to be realistic.

It takes time getting back on track. Education is such a big thing. I just had to keep making short-term plans until I am ready to get into my big plans—it is the only thing I can do. I have to have patience and keep doing the little things, like I finally graduated from high school. I had my child in grade nine and it took me two extra years to graduate but I finally did. There are many ways to reach your goal. I had to ask for help; it's not a bad thing to do. The best thing I did was find out what my options were. I had to look for ways to do things I didn't think I could do. Reaching your goal is about the best thing you can do for yourself. You just have to keep in mind that you have to take baby steps and be patient.

suspended temporarily, because success and failure are not usually determined by how many achievements are checked off the list by a certain age. The positive side of "Indian time" is the freedom to pursue life in a way that fits the individual. The negative side is that, in a majority non-Aboriginal society, a person pursuing a life path outside the norm can feel out of synch.

An exasperated front-line worker said, "I try to tell the young people at the schools that there is an order of things that works best in the modern world. Finish high school, get some training or higher education, get a job and get good at it, then settle down with a husband or wife and have kids. But they don't get it. They see it happening ass-backwards. I tell them, look around. Young people get a girl- or boyfriend, then have a kid, then maybe another one, and then maybe another girl- or boyfriend, then finish high school, then maybe get some training. By that time, they don't know how to get a job and everyone else out there has a whole bunch of experience. God, don't ask me what we need to be doing, but we better do something now or our kids are still going to be left out of the opportunities out there."

Among the young women we talked with, three had had jobs off the reserve during their teen years. For the rest of them, school and child care responsibilities were inhibiting factors, but they also didn't necessarily want to work off the reserve. That was intimidating. They had no experience working with non-Aboriginal people and were afraid they wouldn't be accepted by their co-workers. A lack of confidence to compete in the job market also held them back. In the meantime, they were also much more focused on the easier and more structured task of completing their education, despite the challenges of arranging babysitting, transportation, privacy, and time to study, not to mention dealing with sick babies and, from time to time, new boyfriends.

It can be a struggle for teen mothers not to blame their children for their problems. Motherhood is overwhelming. Many young mothers have times when they wish they could be released from all their responsibilities. For teenagers who have had little or no positive parenting role models, frustration can lead to violence and abuse. Some of the young mothers cried a lot, and got so anxious they could hardly breathe. A few of them admitted to getting angry at their children, something they never thought they would do. Once the young women had experienced what seemed like hours of their baby crying without reprieve, or several nights in a row without more than a few hours of sleep, they often saw themselves acting in ways they had never expected. "I get so tired," one young mom said, "I can hardly control myself.

I love my daughter so much but sometimes I get so frustrated and I get all ballistic on her. It's not her fault that I'm stressed out. I have to remember that and tell her that I'm sorry if I'm acting like a crazy. That's the thing. It's not her fault that life sucks sometimes. When I think about it, she's the good part.

Sometimes I get frustrated that I can't be the mom I want to be. I don't like the way I was raised and I do things differently with my daughter. I want her to have what I never had. I love my mom and all the ladies who had an influence on my life because I think I'm all right but I think the drinking made me do a lot of things I wish I didn't—just like my parents did to me. This is a big problem.

Nobody can ask you to do anything more than your best. Sometimes that's a better job than other times. It's the same with everybody. Young moms shouldn't be too hard on themselves. Most of the time you are your own worst critic. Just love your child. Hug and kiss your child. That's all they ask from you. And then ask for help. It's not always the proudest thing to do but it is the most responsible. Sometimes young moms set too high expectations for themselves and then they have to break their promises. They should just take it day by day. The main thing is to let your child know you are on their team.

I know I shouldn't blame my son but when he won't go to sleep and I haven't slept properly for days sometimes I feel like puking. Then I get out of control. What am I supposed to do?"

The other moms had suggestions: "Make sure he is safe in his crib and then step outside, breathe deep, and don't go back inside until you feel calmer." Another young woman said, "Go for a walk. Pack him up in his stroller. It doesn't matter what time it is. Just get him out of the house, and you. Don't worry if he's crying outside, just keep walking." Someone else emphasized that it's important for young moms to take time to recognize the positive things they do, and not always focus on the negative. The simple things are important, "like taking your child to the park. That's a good thing and you feel good when you do that."

Communication between parent and child was very important to the young women. They wanted their children to be unafraid to ask questions if they didn't understand. They believed that elders should be respected, but that didn't mean that young people shouldn't be allowed to disagree. They considered communication key to gaining understanding. If their daughters were to be safe, they had to know how to say they were afraid. If their sons were to grow up without violence, they had to know how to express their frustrations. And most of all, they wanted their children to be prepared for their own relationships and the sexual demands that would be placed upon them. How were they going to achieve this? By talking to their children. Sitting the kids down and listening to what they had to say.

"If we don't talk to our kids, how will they learn?" one young mom said. "If we don't listen to them, how are we going to learn what they are doing or how they think?"

These young women believe they are part of the healing process taking place in First Nations across the country. They believe there will be opportunities for them and their children that did not exist for their mothers. They see themselves as cycle breakers for the next generation. Some of them had already broken the cycle of addiction. Many of them were the first in their families to graduate from high school or the first to enter post-secondary education. They want to be part of a community that is changing, and they believe they have a lot to offer.

As parents, in spite of their problems with discipline, the young mothers are working determinedly to establish rules for their children. They believe

When I was growing up my mom barely talked to me about anything. She let me do anything I wanted. She didn't tell me about a lot of stuff and I want my son to know about everything—drinking and smoking. I want my son to go down the right road and you have to be there to help them. He has to know that he can ask. My dad said some stuff to me when I was young but I didn't know I could ask him questions. I just accepted what he said and I didn't understand half the time what he was talking about.

I am going to teach my son how to treat girls. I am going to sit him down and talk to him. Moms give their little boys anything they want and I'm not going to let him get away with it. When my boyfriend was growing up his mom did everything for him. He didn't have a father to talk to him and he doesn't know how to act or even think for himself. My boyfriend is so quiet. I want my boy to be able to ask for things and to say the way he feels and what he thinks.

There are a lot of interruptions in your plans and dreams. It took me some time to get on track—some things change and your priorities shift, but you never lose your dreams or your ability to carry on.

that they are setting higher expectations than had been set for them when they were children. They all believe that their children will be more disciplined and better educated than they had been.

These young women are full of youthful optimism, but they also have a mature and adult outlook that comes from experience. It is an outlook that reflects that they are not only teenagers, but mothers, and adults with a good future.

Speaking as Mothers

Some people criticize me because I left my daughter in daycare while I finished high school. Even now, I feel guilty when I have to study and she has to be quiet and watch a movie or something. I think maybe I'm neglecting her because my school work takes so much of my time. But I tell her it's for both of us and she has to help me out. I don't think it will hurt her. In fact I think it's the best way for me to show her how people have to work hard and give up stuff if they want to accomplish their goals.

The one thing I'm working on is that I've moved off the reserve. I have a better living style off the reserve. There is a lot more to offer her. I'm not ashamed of being native, I'm proud of it, but I see a lot of people on the reserve who are not motivated and I don't want my daughter to be around a place where the majority of the people aren't motivated. There's lots on welfare—I just get sick of it. I want my daughter to be around people who are doing something with their lives. I want her to see that as normal. I want her to do the things I couldn't do because we never had the money. I want her to go on school trips—you know how kids get to go to Europe or Australia. I want her to have those kinds of opportunities. Then she'll be able to make a decision for herself about what she wants to do. Then she won't fall into the thinking like everyone else that there is nothing better to do than fall in love.

The thing I want to teach my daughter is that nobody is the same as anybody else. It's not about being the same or different. With my daughter I want her to know there aren't any boundaries because of race. There's nothing to hold you

*back. We got taught that long
enough. I'm going to teach her
that she has the right to do anything she wants to do. Race isn't
going to stop her. Who's going
to teach our children other
than us? People are only going
to treat you equal if you put
it out there. People don't have
time anymore, they don't care
enough to say hey you can do
it, you are as good as me. Why
should they? It's not up to them,
it's up to you. It's not bad anyway to have people look at you
different—so what. I think it's
good to be different.*

*I want my daughter to go
through life and to know she
can do it. She can have a good
shot at it—that she is able to
put in a good effort. If she goes
to school she can learn to add
up numbers and maybe some
day she will be an accountant.
She needs to know that can
happen. I am afraid sometimes
to send her out there. Everybody*

*else—all the other parents are
thirty or thirty-five and I want
to stay home. I think I'm only
twenty and I feel stupid.*

*But then I have to remem-
ber that's my thing. I can't let
that stand in the way of her.
I thought, how is she going to
learn to relate to any of them?
She is as equal as they are. It
was totally my problem. She
walks in with her head up just
like any other kid. I might not
be the same as everybody but I
want her to know she can fight
for what she believes in and be
a woman that demands respect
from people around her.*

*Some people don't hold their
heads up. They walk around
and feel sorry for themselves
and angry about what has happened to them. It's the one thing
we have to teach our kids—they
can be who they want to be.
They don't need to be cocky but
they need self-esteem.*

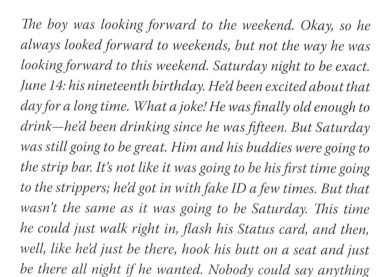

9

We're still teenagers

The boy was looking forward to the weekend. Okay, so he always looked forward to weekends, but not the way he was looking forward to this weekend. Saturday night to be exact. June 14: his nineteenth birthday. He'd been excited about that day for a long time. What a joke! He was finally old enough to drink—he'd been drinking since he was fifteen. But Saturday was still going to be great. Him and his buddies were going to the strip bar. It's not like it was going to be his first time going to the strippers; he'd got in with fake ID a few times. But that wasn't the same as it was going to be Saturday. This time he could just walk right in, flash his Status card, and then, well, like he'd just be there, hook his butt on a seat and just be there all night if he wanted. Nobody could say anything to him.

At least that's the way he had dreamed it would be and the way he wished it still was. The more he thought about it the more he realized that nothing was further from the truth. His girlfriend didn't want him to go. She'd been nagging at him to stay home since his buddies first started planning the night. What else was new? She hated him hanging around

127

with his friends, and if she got her way he wouldn't have any friends at all other than her. He had invited her to come along but that was another joke. She was only seventeen and even if she could get ID they'd have to get a babysitter and she was pregnant again and couldn't drink anyway.

"Fuck her," he said to himself. "She can stay home. It's my birthday and the guys wanna go out."

His friends had been phoning all week like a bunch of schoolgirls. They were as riled up about the weekend as him. They'd been talking about girls mostly—definitely the topic for discussion this week.

The boy looked at his girlfriend, who was sleeping with her head on his lap. The blue light from the TV lit up her cheekbones and jaw so he could see the pretty girl he had been so hot to chase a few years ago. Now that she'd had their son and was almost ready to have number two she was heavier and definitely not as hot as she used to be. He stroked her hair and worried about the feeling in his gut. He'd said he loved her loads of times but that was for her—it seemed to make her happy. The honest truth was he didn't even know what love was, for real. Suddenly he thought the pain in his gut might be love because in spite of all the excitement with his buddies about going out and getting girls this weekend, deep down inside he wanted to stay home and look after his girlfriend and son.

The boy looked at his baby boy sleeping on a mattress beside the sofa. When he looked at the little boy's sleeping face, that's when the boy decided he did know what love was. He wanted to look after his boy if it was the last thing he did. He wanted to be the best father in the world. He thought about when his boy got to be four or five he would take him fishing and hunting. He'd straighten up and go to treatment and stop drinking and show his boy how to be a man. And by then he might have a little girl as well and imagine that.

Nothing felt better than when the boy thought about his children.

The phone rang and he reached across his sleeping girlfriend and answered it. "Yeah, Saturday. Right. You heard? Yeah, everyone's going to be there. Ha. Ha. You got that right." The boy lowered his voice. "Yeah, after the bar? Yeah, line her up for me. It's my birthday, isn't it?"

When he put the receiver down he wanted to phone his best buddy and talk. He felt like someone had tied a knot in his gut and was pulling it tighter with every breath and he needed to tell someone—a guy. But he knew his buddy would laugh and then he would laugh and what good would that do.

For a moment he thought he would just forget the whole Saturday night thing. Write it off. Tell everyone he was sick— not far from the truth given how he was feeling. Yeah, so who gives a shit about Saturday night, he thought, yeah, so what? He felt good thinking about staying home and maybe playing with his son and watching a movie with his girlfriend. They could order in and have a family birthday. But when the phone rang again he could feel Saturday night barrelling down the road like a semi-trailer truck straight toward him. Saturday night was happening, man, there was no two ways about that, it's like he wasn't in control. He had to be there. What could he do?

"Hey, yeah, of course, man. What do you think?" He laughed but he didn't feel like laughing because he was thinking about Sunday and Monday and he didn't like what came to mind. He imagined the wreck he would be and the fight with his girlfriend and the look on his boy's face.

First Nations or not, any teenager who has a baby has her life thrown completely out of order. Teenagers are not supposed to be wiping milk from their breasts in front of their friends, or changing diapers, or staying up all night with a crying baby while their boyfriend is listening to loud music in the next room. Aboriginal teenage mothers do experience a different reality and different circumstances than do non-Aboriginal young women, and they may not be ostracized in their communities for reasons already discussed, but essentially they are in the same boat as any other teenage parent: their way of life has been changed irrevocably.

Being a teenager is hard enough as it is. Life isn't necessarily a voyage of free, fun-loving self-discovery. More likely, it is full of self-doubt, insecurity, and fears about the future. When motherhood is added to that recipe, none of the other ingredients disappear. If anything, the incompatibility of the two states makes both of them worse. That incompatibility—between being a modern teenager and a mother, no matter from what culture—is in simple things: fitting into tight jeans, doing your hair, going out until the early hours of the morning, spending time on the Internet, emailing friends. It is also in more complicated things: getting enough sleep, not having enough time to do everything properly, having no money to buy food and diapers, and not having a stable and private place in which to live and bring up a child.

We wanted a baby. So when I was pregnant I was happy. I didn't know what it would be like. Now I wish we had waited. I shouldn't have had my baby when I was so young but I thought it would be different. Don't get me wrong, I love my baby. I am glad he was born. I never wish he wasn't born. I just wish I had him when I was finished school and in my twenties.

In *Canada's Teens: Today, Yesterday, and Tomorrow,* author Reginald Bibby explores teenage attitudes and practices in such diverse areas as sexuality, nationalism, and spirituality. In a series of extensive surveys Bibby asked teenagers to rate how much they were bothered by various problems. Topping the list were lack of time and money. For the average teenager, that means not having the right clothes or enough time to hang around. For teenage mothers, lack of time and lack of money are both desperate matters.

Teenage motherhood is an instantaneous immersion into the life of an adult—and a life that is far from easy. One day a teenager is obsessing over sexy new low-cut jeans at the mall; the next she is pulling up elastic-waisted sweatpants borrowed from an aunt. She goes from sleeping for twelve hours a day and partying all night to twenty-four-hour child care, with only a few minutes of sleep here and there when the baby gives her a break. Financial support comes from a combination of social assistance, school allowances, child benefits, and, if she is lucky, a part-time job or help from family or her boyfriend. What money there is does not get spent on makeup or new jeans. It pays for diapers, baby food, bus fares, baby clothes, and toys. Luxury becomes a spare hour to hang out with a friend, or read a magazine.

The teenage years are usually a time to develop a sense of identity. It is a time to experiment and test boundaries. But self-development often gets sidetracked by a relationship. "Who am I?" gets superseded by "Who does he want me to be?" Although the young women had all wanted a relationship, most of them subsequently realized that all their attention became concentrated on their boyfriend. His family,

My boyfriend was, like, telling me what to wear. He wanted me to wear all these tight clothes and I used to. After the baby he tried to get me into those clothes and now my style has completely changed. I can finally stand up for myself and nowadays I wear whatever I want.

My boyfriend wouldn't hang out with my friends so I ended up just hanging out with his friends all the time. They were older than me and they weren't my choice of friends. They were totally different.

It's changed everything since I got pregnant. None of my friends like my boyfriend either. I don't hang around much with them anymore. I kind of miss it, especially my cousin. I can't go out with her anymore because my boyfriend doesn't get along with her and a bunch of other people. It's kind of hard on me because I want to go out with them, but at the same time I want him to be there too, so we're just at home all the time with his uncles. I can't do the things I want to do. When I do see my friends and can talk to them they tell me do this and that but at the same time I'm happy.

I have been on my own for a while (separated from my daughter's father) and I'm able to be more focused on my own goals. I'm able to live my life freely. I am able to give my daughter more attention.

his friends, and his interests became their *raison d'être*, at the expense of any sense of self and their own needs and desires.

Once they had a baby, the problem worsened. They didn't like the situation they found themselves in, but they also didn't fight it: they simply now divided their attention between two other people instead of just one. They continued to ignore their own needs. Eventually, the tension became too great, and many of the couples had split up by the time their babies were a year old. Those young women who were not in a relationship seemed to develop a stronger sense of their own well-being than those who were struggling to maintain a relationship. Despite that, they all sought out new relationships to replace the one they had had with their baby's father.

With their girlfriends, it was different. Before the young women became pregnant, their girlfriends had been almost as important to them as their boyfriends. The "girl group" was their second home, a place to talk all day and hang out all night. It was unimaginable that they should no longer be part of the group. But after their babies were born, the young women found themselves automatically putting their personal and social needs and desires after the physical needs of their babies. They had little choice but to do so, whether they liked it or not.

The non-parent friends of the young women didn't set them aside immediately, but it didn't take long for their relationships to change. At first, for example, they had plenty of offers from their friends to babysit. But the offers dried up once the baby arrived: their friends had better things to do than sit around the house watching television and changing diapers.

The young mothers quickly learned whom they could count on, and for most of them it wasn't the friends they had had before they got pregnant. One of the hardest lessons the young women learned was that many of their friends were of the fair-weather variety. Now they had to become friends with each other—not necessarily the people they would naturally have gravitated toward so much as simply people in the same situation.

The greatest regret for the young women we talked with was the loss of freedom to do the simple things: picking up their soccer boots and running to the field without having to think about a babysitter or breastfeeding; saying yes to a coffee invitation without having to plan the outing around sleep times. Spontaneity—or rather, a

When I was pregnant I hung out and did stuff with all my friends. I went to movies and parties. Now the baby is born they stopped calling me. They called me a couple of times after he was born and said oh, I want you to come out with us and I was, like, oh, I can't. After that happened a couple of times they stopped calling completely. Now having the baby takes up all my time.

Most of my friends drank while I was pregnant. I went out too. I went clubbing and did everything until I got to about seven months. Then I stopped. When I stopped going to the clubs they stopped calling me. I was really upset. I didn't know what to do. I was just on my own after that. I just stayed home crying. After my baby was born I still was crying all the time. It was really hard.

lack of it—separated them from their non-parent peers.

Showing a maturity that may have been the product of their hard experience, none of them expressed bitterness or resentment, but merely a sense of grief for a lost youth. They could be seen as simply resigned to their life circumstances, but in fact none of them had given their situation much thought at all. Some of them admitted outright that they had avoided thinking about their lives because they thought "they sucked," and what could they do about it, anyway? On the other hand, some of the girls developed strong ties with other young moms and seemed more content with their new baby-centred lifestyle.

Teenage mothers face parental fears that are common to all mothers: where to live, how to pay the bills, how to feed the baby well, how to keep the baby healthy, someone stealing the baby, losing it somewhere, discovering it has been abused. But unlike older parents, they don't have the skills, experience, or education to deal with those fears. They don't know what is unrealistic. What might be a minor scare to an older mother can be the cause of a complete panic attack for a teenager. While on the one hand ignorance can be bliss—the less you know, the less there is to worry about—the fear factor is still a black dog creeping around the edges of their existence and waiting to attack. Because these young women worried about large and intangible issues out of their control—the kidnapper around the corner, rather than what to make for baby's dinner—fear often immobilized them.

Teenagers are also still, in some respects, children. Girls worry about how big their breasts will grow, and many of them are afraid of the dark. One young woman was too afraid to get up and feed her baby in the middle of the night. The lights in the house were always turned off after she went to bed, so when her baby woke up later on, the house was dark. She would make her boyfriend get up first and turn all the lights on. Another young woman had heard that babies of teen mothers were more likely to die of sudden infant death syndrome, and was too frightened to fall asleep in case her baby died while she wasn't watching. Still another young woman wanted to breastfeed her baby; she knew that breastfeeding was important for her baby's health, and she couldn't afford formula. But she couldn't bring herself to expose her breasts, and she couldn't imagine a baby sucking on them. She was fourteen years old. She hadn't had those breasts very long.

At the same time, the young women did not view themselves in terms of their weaknesses or inadequacies. Most of them said that when they became mothers, they were forced to look at big questions that they might have otherwise avoided. Having a baby gave them a reason to refocus on their personal goals and rethink their priorities. They questioned what sort of people they wanted to be, and how to treat other people. They questioned their own childhoods, and whether their experiences should be recreated in their own parenting style.

They recognized the interruption that had occurred to their normal development as teenagers, and missed being part of their former peer group, but most of them also realized that their friends were not the best influence on them or their babies. Whether for their own sense of self-worth or out of an honest belief in this notion,

The thing I hated the most was waking up in the middle of the night. It was so freaky. Half the time I was awake all night and everyone else in the house was asleep. I'm afraid of the dark and I try not to get out of bed. I just keep the night light on.

It's a relief when your baby starts sleeping all night. But I remember the first night my baby slept through the whole night. By this time I was used to getting up every couple of hours. I woke up after baby was sleeping for a couple of hours and checked her. Then I woke up her dad and asked him to check her every couple of minutes. I couldn't sleep. Then I got too scared to get up and check her. I woke him up again and got him to check if she was still breathing. He said she was, but I stayed awake all night and got him to keep checking her.

I'm going to be there for my daughter. I'm going to show her I'm doing the best I can. A lot of people criticize how I'm raising her—they may not agree with everything I do, but I am raising myself and my daughter and I think we'll be fine. I remember just try and give her as much as I can because when I was younger my mom and dad weren't there for me. There was nobody there to get me what I needed.

My baby straightened me up. Once I was a mom it made me think. School wasn't my main priority until after my son was born. That's when I really knew I had to graduate. I wanted to give him a better life than I had. I wanted him to have a mom that had a job.

It's about how you carry yourself when you're a young mom. You gotta hold your head up and look people in the eye. That's the only way you're going to get any respect from them.

they pictured themselves as having become hard-working and responsible, and distinguished their former peer group members as immature and out of control by comparison. While they suffered from bouts of wishful thinking about being free to come and go as they pleased, they all felt that they had benefited from maturing earlier than their peers. They saw themselves as having a greater understanding of life and a better sense of themselves than their peers. They thought they worked harder and were less selfish than other young women their age. They also thought that having their babies while they were young had taught them a deeper meaning of the word love, and forced them to understand the nature of unquestionable commitment. They had acquired many life skills they might never have had otherwise. Life had ceased to be an aimless journey from nowhere to nowhere, and had taken on real meaning, a state they believed their friends didn't yet share. This didn't amount to self-deception: they really were taking on the attributes they talked about.

These perspectives were hard won. The physical distress of being

a pregnant teenager has been discussed already and cannot be overstated. What's worse for any teenage girl than putting on large amounts of weight suddenly? It was hard enough to feel sick, nauseated, and unfit, but all of the young women quickly started putting on weight when they became pregnant and had to deal with

My body isn't as attractive as it used to be. My health wasn't very good during my pregnancy. It was a very emotional time for me and I didn't have much energy to look after myself. It took me a long time afterwards to get back to normal.

I used to dress up and look good. Now look at me. I'm all slouchy with big T-shirts and sweatpants. That's all that fits now even though baby is almost two years old. This is it, I guess—it's all the weight I'm going to lose.

the pressure of negative self-image and the impact on their relationships with their boyfriends.

Things did not necessarily improve after the baby was born. The weight they gained while they were pregnant was difficult to lose. None of them had money to buy "feel-good" transitional clothing, so they resorted to baggy sweatpants, which didn't help their sense of self-esteem. And, like all new mothers, they didn't have the energy or the inclination to worry about how they looked when they hadn't slept and their babies had used up every bit of energy they could muster. They were also highly emotionally taxed, and not just by their suddenly changed lives. Without the luxury of a patient, understanding partner (their teenage boyfriends were not usually prepared for the physical transformation that took place), the young women were constantly worried that their boyfriends were looking around at other girls.

As noted in Chapter Seven, family reactions were yet another pressure that the teenagers had to manage, ready or not. The problems with lack of family support and an inhospitable home environment have also been discussed. But whether the young women had close relationships with their families or not, it was difficult for them to redefine their place at home. The difficulties are mirrored for the adults. Parents still wanted to treat their daughters like teenagers, while expecting them to act like mothers. All of a sudden their little girl is no longer bursting into the kitchen with news of school or soccer practice, but is heating bottles before bed and packing a stroller and diaper bag.

If teenage girls are unprepared to be mothers, their thirty- or forty-year-old mothers are often just as unprepared to be grandmothers—something that could account for behaviour seen as hostile or counterproductive. One young woman complained that when she tried to say no to her son, for example, her mother always found a way to give him what he wanted. It added confusion to her inexperience: she questioned whether her mother was right and she was constantly doing the wrong thing. While she wondered whether in fact it might be her mother who was wrong, her lack of experience kept her from challenging her mother.

What are new grandparents to do when they hear both their grandchild and daughter crying at the same time? Do they rush in and help? Do they wait and let her take care of it herself? The push-pull creates a great deal of tension in the family. Stand back too much, and the young mothers are left feeling they aren't getting the help they need. Do too much, and grandparents feel they aren't appreciated when they are told to back off—or, if they aren't told to back off, the young mother doesn't develop confidence in her parenting ability. It's almost impossible to know how much help is too much or too little. The level of assistance each young mother needs is different. Some of the young women said when they needed help they were happy to receive it; others said they wanted to prove they could do it all themselves, and knew that at times they resisted assistance even when they desperately needed it. Naturally, that left their parents feeling confused and angry.

My daughter Heather and granddaughter Yetsa lived with me for five years after Yetsa was born. For the first three or four years, I was never sure how to strike the right balance between being there for them and letting them make their own way. I would promise to babysit so that Heather could go out with her friends, and then lie awake wondering if I babysat too much. Was I spoiling her? Should I have said no? If I had said no, would she resent not having the freedom to be a teenager when I could have helped her? On the one hand, I felt I was too lenient. At other times I agonized that I was too strict. Sometimes I felt I had too much control altogether because how her life unfolded seemed to be so closely linked to what I had to say. At the same time, she was fourteen years old: I couldn't simply abdicate responsibility for my child. I never felt that I got the balance right—first too much, then too little, and then too much again—while all the time thinking that either decision was as likely right as wrong.

Heather tells her side of the story like this: "I never knew where I was with Mom. She'd say yes, she'd babysit, and then she'd say I should have stayed home. So instead of going out and having fun, I'd feel guilty all the time, like I was never doing enough. It got so that every time I went out I'd have to ask Mom as if I was a little kid. Then I was always worried that I was putting her out."

Heather and I would both describe our relationship throughout as good, and that the time we spent together while she matured enough to move out on her own was an unqualified success. Yet we both felt compromised and never quite satisfied that we had lived up to our responsibilities.

What would have helped the most on my part was greater flexibility in reassessing my role frequently. I was constantly searching for the right balance, not realizing that there was no right answer—that the best I could do was take it one day at a time. But there were things that I did have, which helped significantly: a home that was large and stable enough to incorporate another little family, and financial security sufficient to cover the cost of another child (which often meant taking time off work to babysit, or paying baby-sitting costs). I was also lucky to have a good relationship with my daughter. Otherwise, the stress of Yetsa's arrival would have been much more difficult to deal with. Many families are not so lucky.

10

OUR RELATIONSHIPS

The girl loves her boyfriend, there is no doubt about it, even though she never thought she would. She's known him since she was a little girl and she never imagined that he would be her boyfriend, but they got together one night and she got pregnant and since then they haven't been apart. He's there for her no matter what. As she phones everyone she can think of, she realizes that he's not the problem at all. The problem for her is his mother and his sisters who won't leave her alone, and now that the baby is born they won't leave him alone, either.

She knows that he's not going to be too pleased with her when he finds out that she has found a basement suite to rent in her auntie's place up the road. He's going to think that she's not grateful and that she doesn't like his family. He might even say he's not moving out, because he always tries so hard to please his mother. But the girl knows that more than anything she wants to have a family of her own. She's going to raise her son different from everyone. And if that's going to happen they need a place of their own.

When the girl's boyfriend comes home she breaks the

news. "I've found us a place of our own." She's right. At first
he says no, he's not moving. It's free at home and if they move
they will have to pay rent. They don't have any furniture.
Who will babysit when they want to go out? And what about
his mother, she'll be hurt? What about the bills? How will
they pay the bills? He has every reason in the book why they
should stay with his family.

"I love you," the girl says. "There's no doubt about it." But
she tells him that she's found out she loves her baby, too, and
just as much. She tells him about her plan for the baby and
how she wants their baby to grow up. "So," she says, "the only
way that's going to happen is if we take care of him ourselves.
It'll be hard, I know, but we can do it."

She isn't sure her boyfriend believes her but he knows
she means what she says. It will be hard telling his mother
and sisters. They don't like her much anyway. And, just like
he said, it will be hard paying the bills and having no help
around. But one thing the girl is certain of: maybe she is only
seventeen, but she is a mother now and has a family. No one
is going to take that away from her.

Teen families are formed out of circumstance, rarely out of love or choice. The babies born to teen parents cannot generally be called "love children." Only four of the young women mentioned love when they talked about their boyfriends. The rest had their partner chosen for them by their pregnancy, and once they realized they shared a lifelong commitment with their boyfriend, they decided to try to stick it out together. They wanted a father for their baby, or they didn't want to "fail" twice: they wanted to prove that the whole thing wasn't a mistake. These are not sound bases on which to build a family, and most teen relationships don't last.

Of the thirteen young women, two remained single and lived at home with their parents after their baby was born. One lived with her family along with her boyfriend. The rest moved into the boyfriend's house. That was not a simple choice of where to live based on which family had room for them; there appeared to be more complicated underlying reasons involved. What do you do when you have a baby and are sixteen years old, 20 kilograms overweight, breastfeeding, tired and grumpy, and plagued by the fear that your boyfriend is looking at other girls? You find ways to hold on. Sometimes, you compromise what is best for you and your baby in order to please your boyfriend.

Once I got pregnant we thought we were going to have the perfect family. But after we had the baby we soon realized things would never be the same. Now we are separated and we both still think about how great life was before, when it was just the two of us. We think about how much fun and love we had. But life goes on. I wish we had waited and been able to have that fun for a while longer— that young love I'm not sure I'll ever have again.

Living at the boy's house means he has less to give up. He gets to live with his family and be close to his friends. That way he is more likely to come home, at least some of the time. But the young women who lived at their boyfriends' houses often hardly knew his family, and it wasn't easy to feel comfortable. Even if they were supported by the boy's mother, more often than not the boyfriend's siblings resented their presence. Most of the homes the young women moved into were already overcrowded, which meant displacement of other family members. Tensions were often high. While the young women did what they could to try to fit in, their efforts didn't always work. They wanted to help with meals and chores, but didn't know what was expected of them. More often than not they felt they were just getting in the way, so they spent most of their time in their bedroom with their boyfriends and their babies and with the door shut.

It's kind of crappy living under someone else's roof because then they can make rules and you have no other choice. If you don't like the rules then you have to go find someplace else to live. That makes it really hard, because not many people want a small family moving in with them; they probably have enough people in their house already. It makes it harder to find a place. Then when you try and look for a place on your own it's too hard because you have to have a lot of money.

I don't like my boyfriend's family. I don't like the way they raise their kids. I don't trust them. A lot of stuff has gone on in their family. The only person in the house I trust is my boyfriend and his sister. I have to spend every minute with my baby to make sure she is safe.

Many of the couples had known each other only a few months when the young woman became pregnant. Before they really had a chance to get to know each other, all of a sudden she is suffering from morning sickness and then gaining weight. Then she moves into her boyfriend's family home, where his family is cool if not outright difficult. So she stays in his room that has a closet, a dresser, a double bed, and a television set. When the baby comes, she stuffs a crib next to the bed. Everyone in the family can hear every argument because the walls are paper thin and there is always someone around listening. Everyone knows everything. It's not surprising that many teen parent relationships look more like desperation than love and commitment.

Don Burnstick, a First Nations comedian, quips that First Nations men don't get girlfriends; they take hostages. But while initially a young man may possessively and aggressively claim a young woman's attention, after she has their baby, she in turn may start demanding his full and exclusive attention, to the detriment of both. One young woman, feeling dislocated, insecure, and crushed by responsibility, wouldn't let her boyfriend out of her sight. She had lost enough; she wasn't going to lose her boyfriend, too.

One grandfather described how his son's relationship has prevented him from getting ahead in his life: "He was seventeen years old when his girlfriend had the first baby. He didn't even graduate. As soon as his girl got pregnant, she held onto him like he was on a leash. He didn't get up for a cup of coffee without her asking him where he was going. Once the baby was born he had to be with the mom and his daughter all the time. I mean every minute. I tried to get him to get up and go to school but no, she'd cry when he wasn't there with her. I've been telling him to get a job but now the second baby's coming along. He's almost twenty and he still hasn't got a job."

His son is not alone. Many of the young men we spoke to said that when they first got together with their girlfriends they were with each other "24/7," until they suffocated each other. A common problem with teen parents is that instead of the family having two working parents, or even one working parent and one stay-at-home parent, they become a family with two stay-at-home parents. "We gotta do something about it. Young people think it's normal," said the same grandfather. "Too many of our young men hang around with their girlfriends and babies for so long that they get too scared to go out and look for their first job. They need to be doing that when they are in their teens, not when they're twenty-five or so."

The young relationships often became a series of negotiations about who should be doing what, who gets to go out, and who has to stay in. Most of the young women were at the losing end of the negotiations, but that didn't necessarily mean the young men were free of feeling trapped. The young mothers resented their boyfriends' freedom to go to the bathroom or take a shower alone; it seemed unfair. They felt if they were stuck, then he should feel stuck, too. Why should their boyfriends be able to walk out of the house to visit friends, or go to a party on Friday night, while they had to stay home? It is a question that created enormous tension between the young couples, and that they often could not resolve.

The young women were afraid because they knew what goes

My boyfriend was happy when I got pregnant. I even heard that he told one of his friends that now I'm pregnant he won't have to worry about anyone wanting to screw around with me. He said no one would want me now, so he didn't have to worry about me anymore. But he still goes out and I've heard that he's screwing around.

Now since I got pregnant I'm too afraid to have sex. Even though I'm on birth control now I just don't want to take the chance. My boyfriend doesn't get it.

When I go out with some guy I can tell he doesn't want to have a baby. Guys can't see past that he's going to have to be some kind of dad. I tell them I'm not looking for a dad for my baby but it scares them off. Then there are other guys that love babies. They say they want babies. That kind of scares me off.

on at parties: "everyone looking at everyone, getting together with anyone." One young mother's experience was typical. "After the party, this chick comes over and starts telling me all kinds of stories about who was with who and who was looking at who," she said. "She knew I was freaking out about my boyfriend. She just loved it." Even the relationships that started out well were almost immediately in trouble with jealousy, resentment, and anger. Frustration resulting from undeveloped and unequal relationships was rife.

Not surprisingly, with all these pressures on their relationships, few of the young women ended up staying with the fathers of their babies. Some of the couples separated after a few months; others lasted a few years.

Once separated, a few of the young women avoided the dating scene and focused on their education and baby. Most, however, were also interested in a new relationship. Young mothers want to feel attractive, to believe that they can still get a boyfriend. Unfortunately, as one young woman said, "You bring a lot of baggage into a relationship when you have a kid, starting with a diaper bag." Babies, especially someone else's, aren't necessarily an asset for a young woman looking for a new relationship. Most teenage males aren't interested in becoming fathers, let alone stepfathers.

In one sense, these young women were even more compromised in their approach to dating someone new than they had been with their previous boyfriends. They were just as eager to please their new boyfriends, if not more. They knew that once a boy realizes she can't go to all the parties because she doesn't have a babysitter, and that she can't drink because she is breastfeeding or she can't sleep over at his house because she has to get home to her baby, he may soon decide she isn't such a good catch. Torn between desires and responsibilities, and with little or no money, they don't always make the best decisions. They might leave the baby in unsuitable child care arrangements, or not come home when promised, or sleep in and not feed the baby breakfast.

A few young women had one boyfriend followed by another and another. Their greatest fear was being alone, and it was a greater fear than any they might have had of being in a bad relationship. Consequently, they had a series of bad relationships.

All the young women worried about how a new boyfriend would

Other guys think just because I've had a baby that I'm going to be easy and want sex all the time. They're stupid. I'm, like, forget it—I don't want it now I have a baby—it's the opposite.

The one thing I am having a lot of trouble with is that I need to have a guy around. It's like an addiction. I know it's not good for my kids but when my ex left I needed someone, bad. I wasn't alone for very long but in the middle of the night a guy came to my door and said, "I'm coming in to be with you tonight." I was so alone. I told him no way, get out of here. But I had to force myself to do it. When I got with my current boyfriend I wanted him to stay. When it came time for him to go at night I would hang on and not let him go. I want to break that cycle. I know that about myself now. I have broken a lot of other cycles and I'll break that one too. I want to be able to be alone and be okay with it.

I'm not about to bring dates home to meet my daughter. Forget it. Some guy was, like, "I'll take you and your daughter out," and I'm, like, "She hasn't got anything to do with you."

You have to go slow. I didn't even let my daughter meet my new boyfriend until I knew him pretty good. Then it was only when I was around.

I think you gotta let your boyfriend meet your kid early in the relationship because what happens if your kid doesn't like him or you don't like the way he treats your kid. You better find that out right away, like before you fall in love with him.

I had to go really slowly. My youngest was really jealous of me when their father left. Whenever my boyfriend came over she would sit close to me and watch everything he did. He couldn't even put his arm around me without her getting jealous.

affect their children. They were wary of stepfathers, and unsure of how to protect their children from the young men around them. While they might have been attracted to a young man, or felt good about his attention, they rarely thought he or his friends were good for their children, and they watched the children conscientiously.

Even with a good new boyfriend, there were complications. It was difficult to know when to introduce the boyfriend to the child. Some felt it was important to get to know him very well first; others thought it was important to see how he related to the child right away. One young woman said the baby's father got jealous because of her new boyfriends, and that "it's like he thinks he owns me because I have his baby. He wants to fight them all the time. I can't even go out with anyone without him sticking his nose in on it." Another said that it was her child who was jealous of her shared affections.

On the other hand, the relationship between new boyfriend and child could end up going too well. As one young woman said, "It complicates all your relationships. One of my boyfriends fell in love

All I have to worry about is that my son is here on earth with me. I want to grow him up well and love him and be there for him. I just need a little more time and we will be one of the best families in the world. I want my son to grow up knowing he has great parents.

My ex takes care of our daughter. He's pretty good now that she's three. But it's always on his terms. If he knows I really need him it seems like he deliberately finds something else to do.

The thing that really gets me mad is that whenever my ex takes our daughter out or gives her something everyone says what a great guy he is. Oh, wasn't that wonderful, he spent time with his daughter. I'm with her every day, no one says that about me. Why is he suddenly the hero just because he takes her to a movie?

with my daughter, too—it was so hard for him to break up with me because he missed her so much. He still wants to buy her birthday gifts and Christmas gifts."

A few young women kept focused on their goal to form a family with the father of their child. In spite of complicated circumstances they did whatever it took to create a household. One mother said she didn't like her in-laws and refused to let them babysit or have any input into her baby's life whatsoever. She lived with them as long as she had to, but once a mobile home became vacant she moved her family out on their own. "I had to stick with it for a year and it wasn't easy," she said. "It was hard on my boyfriend because I couldn't get along with his family and they were insulted because I wanted to move out as soon as possible. But we're through it now and we're still together. Now we can do things our way."

Even those young women enjoying relatively good relationships didn't feel they had equal partnerships. They felt as though they were the ones putting in all the work. In every case, the young women were the primary caregivers for the babies, and the fathers' contributions were voluntary, arbitrary, and often non-existent. Despite that, the young women seemed to think that they should feel grateful for anything they could get. They weren't giving up.

A few of the young men stepped up to the plate and became committed fathers and partners. Some were great fathers even if they weren't living with the mothers. They visited their babies, played with them, even took them for the weekend, although the visits were always at the fathers' convenience. Other separated fathers were less than reliable when it came to sharing in child care.

The financial crisis is a huge strain on these young women's relationships. A common assumption in our society is that young people have babies as an easy way to get financial support in the form of social assistance and child benefits. That may be true for a small number of people, but none of these young women wanted to be dependent, broke, or limited to the prospect of being poor for the rest of their lives. In fact, the low income provided by government benefits motivated some of them to finish school and get a job. None of them thought there was anything wrong with receiving social assistance if they were unable to support their baby, but only to fill in the gap, not as a long-term plan.

Being broke, for most of the young moms, taught them to be resource-

So on Friday night, my ex says he's going to take our daughter and I'm going to meet him at the mall. I phone him from the store and he says he's driving away because he had to go pick up a friend. I'm, like, what about our daughter? Sorry, he says, he has other things to do. I'm supposed to be going out and I'm standing there, like, okay, now what do I do. People are waiting for me. It took me until half the night was over until I caught up with him. I missed going out with my friends. Then I'm, like, where are you going with her? He's got friends in the car and I'm freaking about what he's going to do. He gets mad and says it's none of my business. I'm, like, just let me take her home.

I can honestly say I have been poor before but I have never been as broke as I am now I am on my own with my baby. I am dead poor.

Not having enough money can put a strain on your social life. I don't look at it that way. I put money on bills and groceries and then buy the kids the things they need and if I have anything left I go out and do something. When it comes to doing things with your child there are things to do like go to the park that don't cost anything.

When you have your first child, you want it to have everything, especially everything you never had. But then there is reality—you can't afford it. Other than very basic living expenses there isn't any other money. I worried about everything. What about the diapers? What about her formula? What about wipes? She grew so fast she needed new clothes all the time. And what about money for laundry? That doesn't even mention her allergies she got as she got older. A special diet didn't fit into my budget, but I had to make it fit. No wheat products, no citrus. She had to have soy or rice. So a loaf of bread is about a dollar and a loaf of soy bread costs about six dollars. Then her formula cost more too.

ful, something they knew they could use later in life. "If nothing else," one young mom said, "I know how to fend for myself. I know how to make my money go further than I ever thought I could. Sometimes we actually go without things we need but I find ways to get by. My boyfriend always wants to spend money on miscellaneous stuff and I have to say no. We get into fights about it but what can I do?"

For separated moms, receiving child support from the father is not something that can be counted upon. Of the majority of the young women who were not living with the fathers of their babies, only one had received any child support. After a court decision, the young man was ordered to pay sixty dollars per month in financial support. She thought it should have been higher, but it was better than nothing, and she was excited to get the money. Her boyfriend gave her the first cheque on the day of the court decision. The second month was a different story. A week after the agreed-upon payment date, she still didn't have the money, so she telephoned him. He said he was a little short and would soon get her the money. After a few more calls they agreed to meet on a Friday night at seven o'clock. She dressed up, promised to pay the babysitter, and headed out. This was going to be the best Friday night in a long time. But he never showed up. Each month after that she received more empty promises, until finally she stopped telephoning, and then stopped expecting to get the money altogether.

A lawyer told another young woman that she would get less than twenty dollars per month from the father of her child, so she didn't pursue the matter. The others also believed it was futile to pursue their babies' fathers for financial support. Without assistance, the task of pursuing money with a low probability of winning in the end is too daunting a task. The young mothers were also busy with the immediate tasks of child care and didn't think chasing their ex was a practical place to put the time and energy that was needed for their babies—and for themselves.

For these young mothers, dreams of a better life in the future become more important than the past and, to some extent, even more important than the present. What that future holds for them, however, is still far from certain.

Conclusion: Looking Forward

The girl carefully brushes her daughter's hair and twists two perfect braids on either side. She ties blue bows to the ends and leans back. Her daughter is beautiful.

The girl is proud of her daughter. For five years they have walked side by side through the middle of life. It hasn't been easy but they have always been on the same team. The girl and her daughter were defence, offence, and goalie at the same time. The girl's baby went to the school daycare so that the girl could graduate. Now the girl's family helps look after her daughter so the girl can work night shift at a downtown restaurant. The girl's daughter stays quiet in the morning so the girl can sleep. Her daughter knows that later her mom will take her out, maybe to the mall or the park—it'll be just the two of them.

The girl thinks about their life together up to now. She remembers how disappointed her family was when she got pregnant. She remembers returning to school and the look on her teachers' faces when they said something like, "We were shocked when we heard you had a baby." She remembers crying late at night when she was studying for an exam but her brain was mush. She remembers how disappointed she was with herself when she barely passed. She remembers sitting in the emergency room while her daughter burned with a fever and coughed and choked. She was terrified of words like meningitis and asthma and diabetes and the thousands of other words she didn't know but that she knew lurked around doctors' offices and hospital wards. She remembers the frowns and whispers of old ladies and teenagers when she struggled to drag the stroller, diaper bag, and baby on the bus. She remembers walking across the stage of the conference centre in high heels, an evening gown, and a tiara and the tears in the principal's eyes when he placed her diploma in her hand.

Today everything floods back into her brain. Her eyes are clouded with tears when she turns her daughter toward the mirror and says, "Today, baby, it's your turn. Your first day of school." The girl looks into her daughter's face and sees pure, unrestrained joy. Her daughter has wanted to go to school since the day she could want to do anything. "Mommy, when do I get my own school like you?" The girl knows her daughter is bright; she memorized the alphabet when she was three and now she can add and subtract. Her daughter loves to play with children and behaves herself around adults. When the girl looks at her daughter the girl is sure there is nothing that identifies her as the child of a teenager. In spite of what people say and write, her daughter doesn't look any more likely than any other child to be a criminal, get sick, have malnutrition, fail at school, or fail to thrive.

But the girl feels a familiar old fear grip her stomach. She's not hungry and she's hungry at the same time. The girl knows they have to get going but she wants to step back into the house instead of out the door. The girl wishes her mother were there, or her auntie. She wishes she had someone to stand behind.

The girl's eyes move from her daughter up the mirror to her own face. She has carefully applied makeup and tied her hair back in a tight roll. She's wearing loose khaki capris, a cream-coloured T-shirt, and sandals. The girl has done everything to make her nineteen years look like twenty or even twenty-one. But as she examines her face she knows most people will think she's younger.

The girl knows the other parents at the kindergarten will be at least twenty-five or thirty or thirty-five. At the registration open house they looked as old as her own mother. One of them asked the girl if she was babysitting, and another said, "Oh, isn't it nice that you are bringing your sister to school." The girl tried to be polite, but how can you say "No, she's my daughter" without giving away your life story? She could tell from the look on the other mothers' faces that they weren't very impressed with her kind of story. They smiled briefly but then backed away and faced each other.

The girl takes a deep breath. She watches in the mirror as her body grows taller. She stares into her deep brown eyes and feels a gathering in her soul. She remembers other moments in her life when she wanted to crawl inside her body instead of taking her body outside. She remembers her own words, the ones she said the first time she took her baby into the local grocery store and the first time she walked through her high school with her baby. They were the words she said under her breath each time she walked into the world that seemed so unkind and so unfriendly and so ready to judge her and find her guilty of some gross indecency. "Hold your head up, girl," she says out loud. "No one hands you respect on a platter. You have to show them you deserve it."

Then the girl turns back to her daughter and says, "Baby, this is the day you've been waiting for. You give it to them, girl."

The conversation is over and the question is, of course, where do we go from here? With every challenge there is an opportunity to show ingenuity, and the issue of teen parents in First Nations is no exception. Aboriginals and non-Aboriginals alike must commit to provide assistance to and create opportunities for teen parents and their children. It is the only way to offset the effects of poverty and turn the tide on the trend toward younger and younger parents.

Looking from the outside, as we have seen, the prevalence of First Nations teen families is likely the result of a complex combination of historical and community conditions. These are issues that can be addressed only by a commitment from all levels of government to address policy issues and provide financial assistance.

Looking from the inside, it appears that First Nations young women and men have babies for other reasons: many of their friends are having babies, they don't know that there are other opportunities or they don't know how to access them, they don't have the right information to prevent pregnancy, they don't know they can make the choice not to have sex, and no one expects anything else from them, including themselves. These are things First Nations leaders and communities can change.

It's everyone's responsibility to make children once again the priority, in Aboriginal and non-Aboriginal communities alike. Both need to adopt more community programs, such as recreational sports, reading groups, dances, art classes, and cultural activities—all ways for young people to be occupied in healthy ways. When children are the priority, teen moms will be a focus of community attention not just because of their own special needs as children-having-children, but because they bear the gift of life and because, like First Nations mothers throughout history, they will determine the cultural strength of the next generation. If First Nations are to become strong communities with children a priority, teen moms and their children cannot be left to sink or swim according to the strength of their own resources or lack thereof.

If I could say something about the whole thing of being a teenage mom it would be that it all depends on how much help you get. That doesn't mean having someone doing stuff for you all the time. It means knowing you are not alone and when you get totally frustrated and scared that you know there is someone who will step in for you. Your kid needs to know there are people who will be there for him or her too. It's hard work to make a family when you are only fifteen or so but it's not like it can't be done, as long as there is lots of help.

The challenge for non-Aboriginal people and governments is to back up commitments First Nations make to build the capacity and self-esteem of their children. And as Canadians in all walks of life we must do away with our complacency and refusal to acknowledge the pits of poverty that set apart most First Nations reserves as places of disadvantage. Yet the current trend in government policy is to sacrifice social programs in favour of the strictly financial bottom line. I am not an economist, but I believe it is simply good logic to pay the short-term costs of providing services and creating opportunities for teen parents and their children. Getting them on their feet while they are young leads to long-term savings in services not needed later when they lead independent and productive lives. There is false economy in letting small problems become big ones, and nowhere is this more evident than in the lives of underprivileged children. Reductions to social programs rest on the backs of the poorest people in the country—in this case First Nations children and their parents.

Even though more help is desperately needed, conditions are changing in First Nations. Projects such as this one are not uncommon. On every front—education, health, housing, economic development—First Nations are taking new and invigorated approaches to moving their communities from merely surviving to thriving. There's a long way to go, and it's critical that young families, currently stretched to the limit, are part of the revival. We hope that this book will help, both by bringing more awareness to the issues and by offering the perspectives of the young people themselves.

Our project is over but we are still seeing positive outcomes. One was the collaboration between us and the young mothers on a booklet called *Teenagers with Babies: a Discussion for Teenagers with Saanich First Nations Teenage Mothers*. The booklet is widely used in local First Nations communities.

Near the end of the study, three of the participants gave a presentation on teenage parenthood at an international conference at the University of Victoria. Since then they have led discussions at two workshops in local high schools. No doubt there will be more such initiatives.

The thirteen young women are going to school, having more babies, working, struggling, surviving, and thriving. One young woman is in her second year of nursing; another is graduating from high school at the age of twenty-six after having three daughters while she was still a teenager. Another young woman has moved out of the country and set up a new family with her son in a foreign city. She says she misses home but is working and learning about the world in a way she never thought possible. Another young woman is having her second baby since the project. Soon she will have three children, but she is working on her relationship with the children's father, selling cosmetics from her home, and taking computer classes at night. Still another young woman has finally left a destructive relationship and is upgrading at the adult education centre. Her son is currently living with his grandmother, but she hopes to have a place of her own soon and then be reunited with her child.

They all say the project helped them put their lives into perspective. They don't want people to feel sorry for them. They want people to understand that they are working hard against the odds. They also want people to become involved in making children and families a priority. It's not okay that their children live at risk or that there is so much poverty in their communities. The young mothers are doing what they can. And if we help them and teach them skills when they are young and their lives are most unmanageable, then they can do a lot more as they mature.

This project was about talking to one another. Just ask us, the girls said, and let us just ask you, and together we can learn from and understand each other. Women have been talking to each other and gaining strength from each other since forever. Unfortunately, it's becoming rarer to sit down and share our stories. We are sharing our conversation with you, not because we came up with all the answers, but because we believe that people who are part of the conversation will work together to change policies, develop programs, create opportunities, shift community attitudes, and gradually improve the lot of young parents and their children.

Closing Thoughts

I just hope people read this book. Especially young women. They will know they aren't alone. It's so good to know that someone is telling our story. Maybe people will look at us different after this. They might understand us a little better and know how hard it is. There's a lot to do to help teenage moms and their kids, but it's not like we aren't trying.

I don't want people to feel sorry for us. We don't need that. I want people to understand and then maybe look at us different. Then they'll know that we're working hard to make it work for our kids.

I hate reading all those statistics about First Nations kids and how bad off they are. Every time I read them I think it makes it worse. That's all people think about us. It's not true.

We're trying to give our kids the best life we can. It's hard but it's not all bad. We need help when our families are little, but after a while we can make it on our own.

I want to tell you how much I think this research will not only help future young women, but how it has helped all of us. Now we know we are not alone in our experiences. I have enjoyed being able to speak about my life in a safe and open atmosphere. It's not done enough. We come from an oral tradition, yet it takes such a lot of time and dedication to actually connect with each other. Although written material can be effective, I think it will be group situations such as ours that will help future young people understand the true responsibilities of parenthood.

Bibliography

Adams, Howard. *Prison of Grass: Canada from a Native Point of View.* Saskatoon: Fifth House Publishers, 1975.

Anderson, Kim, and Bonita Lawrence. *Strong Women Stories: Native Vision and Community Survival.* Toronto: Sumach Press, 2003.

Anderson, Kim, et al. *Tenuous Connections: Urban Aboriginal Youth Sexual Health and Pregnancy.* Toronto: Ontario Federation of Indian Friendship Centres, 2002. Pdf document available at http://www.ofifc.org/.

Armitage, Andrew. "Lost Vision: Children and the Ministry for Children and Families." *BC Studies.* No. 18, Summer 1998.

Artz, Sibylle. *Sex, Power, and the Violent School Girl.* Toronto: Trifolium Books, 1998.

Bibby, Reginald W. *Canada's Teens: Today, Yesterday, and Tomorrow.* Toronto: Stoddart Publishing, 2001.

Blackstock, Cindy, et al. *Keeping the Promise: The Convention on the Rights of the Child and the Lived Experiences of First Nations Children and Youth.* First Nations Child and Family Caring Society of Canada, April 2004. Pdf document available at http://www.fncfcs.com/docs/KeepingThePromise.

British Columbia Vital Statistics Agency. *Analysis of Health Statistics for Status Indians in British Columbia, 1991–1998.* BC Ministry of Health and Ministry Responsible for Seniors, for the First Nations and Inuit Health Branch, Health Canada, 2000.

British Columbia Vital Statistics Agency. *Analysis of Health Statistics for Status Indians in British Columbia, 1991–1999.* BC Ministry of Health and Ministry Responsible for Seniors, for the First Nations and Inuit Health Branch, Health Canada, 2001.

Carter, Sarah. *Capturing Women: The Manipulation of Cultural Imagery in Canada's Prairie West.* Montreal and Kingston: McGill–Queen's University Press, 1997.

Crey, Ernie, and Suzanne Fournier. *Stolen from Our Embrace: The Abduction of First Nations Children and the Restoration of Aboriginal Communities.* Vancouver: Douglas and McIntyre, 1997.

Dunnett, Janet. "University and Community Linkages at the University of Victoria: Towards a New Agenda for Community Based Research." Unpublished paper. Victoria, BC: University of Victoria, 2004.

During, Alan Thein, and Christopher D. Crowther. *Misplaced Blame: The Real Roots of Population Growth.* Seattle: Northwest Environment Watch. Report No. 5, July 1997.

Feuz, Karen. *Enabling Communities to Respond to the Needs of Young Women at Risk.* Vancouver: BC Task Force on Teen Pregnancy and Parenthood, 1989.

Four Directions Consulting Group. *Implications of First Nations Demography.* Final Report for Indian and Northern Affairs Canada, August 1997. http://www.ainc-inac.gc.ca/pr/ra/execs/index_e.html.

Garrett, Susan Corona, and Romeria Tidwell. "Differences Between Adolescent Mothers and Nonmothers: An Interview Study." *Adolescence.* Vol. 34, No. 133, Spring 1999.

Geronimus, Arline T. "The Effects of Race, Residence, and Prenatal Care on the Relationship of Maternal Age to Neonatal Mortality." *American Journal of Public Health.* Vol. 76, No. 12, December 1986.

Gibbs, Nancy. "The Vicious Cycle." *Time Magazine,* June 20, 1994. http://www.time.com/time/archive/.

Hancock, Emily. *The Girl Within: A Groundbreaking New Approach to Female Identity.* New York: Fawcett Columbine Books, 1989.

Hanna, Barbara. "Negotiating Motherhood: The Struggles of Teenage Mothers." *Journal of Advanced Nursing.* Vol. 34, No. 4, May 2001.

Hardy, Janet B., and Anne K. Duggan. "Teenage Fathers and the Fathers of Infants of Urban, Teenage Mothers." *American Journal of Public Health.* Vol. 78, No. 7, July 1988.

Hubler, Shawn. "Just the Facts of Life Now." *Los Angeles Times,* April 23, 2005. http://www.latimes.com/.

Kaplan, Elaine Bell. *Not Our Kind of Girl: Unraveling the Myths of Black Teenage Motherhood.* Los Angeles: University of California Press, 1997.

Kenny, Janet W., et al. "Ethnic Differences in Childhood and Adolescent Sexual Abuse and Teenage Pregnancy." *Journal of Adolescent Health.* Vol. 21, No. 1, 1997.

King, Thomas. *The Truth About Stories: A Native Narrative.* Toronto: House of Anansi Press, 2003.

Lawson, Annette, and Deborah L. Rhode, editors. *The Politics of Pregnancy: Adolescent Sexuality and Public Policy.* New Haven: Yale University Press, 1993.

Leadbeater, Bonnie J. Ross, and Niobe Way, editors. *Urban Girls: Resist-*

ing Stereotypes, Creating Identities. New York: New York University Press, 1996.

Marshall, Peter. Now I Know Why Tigers Eat Their Young: Surviving a New Generation of Teenagers. Vancouver: Whitecap Books, 2000.

Maynard, Rebecca A., editor. Kids Having Kids: Economic Costs and Social Consequences of Teen Pregnancy. Washington, DC: The Urban Institute Press, 1996.

Miller, Shelby H. Children as Parents: Final Report on a Study of Childbearing and Child Rearing Among 12- to 15-Year-Olds. New York: Child Welfare League of America, 1983.

Office of the Assistant Secretary for Planning and Evaluation. Second Chance Homes: Providing Services for Teenage Parents and Their Children. Report of the US Department of Health and Human Services, October 2000. http://aspe.hhs.gov/hsp/2ndchancehomes00/.

Pipher, Mary. Reviving Ophelia: Saving the Selves of Adolescent Girls. New York: Ballantine Books, 1995.

Polit, Denise F., and Janet R. Kahn. "Early Subsequent Pregnancy Among Economically Disadvantaged Teenage Mothers." American Journal of Public Health. Vol. 76, No. 2, February 1986.

Rickel, Annette U. Teen Pregnancy and Parenting. New York: Hemisphere Publishing, 1989.

Rosenwald, Priscilla R., and Gwen Porter. "Wee Care: Reaching Teenage Mothers and Changing Lives." Children Today. Vol. 18, No. 3, May–June 1989.

Rubin, Lillian B. Worlds of Pain: Life in the Working-Class Family. New York: Basic Books, 1976.

Simmons, Rachel. Odd Girl Out: The Hidden Culture of Aggression in Girls. Orlando: Harcourt Trade Publishers, 2002.

Strauch, Barbara. The Primal Teen: What the New Discoveries About the Teenage Brain Tell Us About Our Kids. New York: Anchor Books, 2003.

Sugar, Max, editor. Adolescent Parenthood. New York: SP Medical and Scientific Books, 1984.

Trad, Paul V. "Assessing the Patterns That Prevent Teenage Pregnancy." Adolescence. Vol. 34, No. 133, Spring 1999.

Van Kirk, Sylvia. "Many Tender Ties": Women in Fur-Trade Society, 1670–1870. Winnipeg: Watson and Dwyer Publishing, 1980.

White, Emily. Fast Girls: Teenage Tribes and the Myth of the Slut. New

York: Scribner, 2002.

Wodarski, Lois A., and John S. Wodarski. *Adolescent Sexuality: A Comprehensive Peer/Parent Curriculum.* Springfield, Illinois: Charles C. Thomas Publisher, 1995.

Wolf, Anthony E. *Get Out of My Life, but First Could You Drive Me and Cheryl to the Mall?: A Parent's Guide to the New Teenager.* New York: Farrar, Straus and Giroux, 2002.

Wood, Robert G., and John Burghardt. *Implementing Welfare Reform Requirements for Teenage Parents: Lessons From Experience in Four States.* Report by Mathematica Policy Research for the Office of the Assistant Secretary for Planning and Evaluation, US Department of Health and Human Services, October 31, 1997. http://aspe.hhs.gov/ hsp/isp/teepareq/front.htm.

WEBSITES

Aboriginal Healing Foundation
http://www.ahf.ca/newsite/

Avert
http://www.avert.org/

Center for AIDS Prevention Studies
http://www.caps.ucsf.edu/

Indian and Northern Affairs Canada
http://www.ainc-inac.gc.ca/index_e.html

National Campaign to Prevent Teen Pregnancy
http://www.teenpregnancy.org/

SIECUS (Sexuality Information and Education Council of the United States)
http://www.siecus.org/

Statistics Canada
http://www.statcan.ca/

Vanier Institute of the Family
http://www.vifamily.ca/

ALSO BY SYLVIA OLSEN

No Time to Say Goodbye

Children's Stories of Kuper Island Residential School

No Time to Say Goodbye is a fictional account of five children sent to aboriginal boarding school, based on the recollections of a number of Tsartlip First Nations people. Taken by government agents from Tsartlip Day School to live at Kuper Island Residential School, the children are isolated on the small island and life becomes regimented by the strict school routine. They experience the pain of homesickness and confusion while trying to adjust to a world completely different from their own. Their lives are no longer organized by fishing, hunting and family, but by bells, line-ups and chores. In spite of the harsh realities of the residential school, the children find adventure in escape, challenge in competition, and camaraderie with their fellow students.

$9.95 • pb • 1-55039-121-6

★ Adopted by the B.C. Teachers' Federation
★ Saskatchewan Young Readers' Snow Willow Award Nominee

White Girl

Fourteen-year-old Josie finds herself living on a reserve outside town, after her mother marries Martin, "a real ponytail Indian," and now she has a new stepfather and stepbrother, and a new name, "Blondie."

"Following her highly acclaimed *Girl with a Baby*, Olsen scores another winner . . . *White Girl* is an outstanding story on may levels, a much-needed addition to the body of contemporary Indian literature for teens."
— *Starred review, School Library Journal*

$9.95 • pb • 1-55039-147-X • Ages 12+

★ Sheila A. Egoff Children's Literature Prize nominee
★ Saskatchewan Young Readers' Choice Snow Willow Award
★ Starred review BOOKLIST

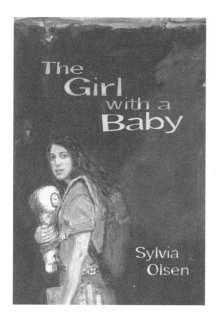

The Girl with a Baby

"This contemporary novel beautifully blends a realistic story of teenage life with a unique view of an old and largely unknown Native culture. This is a common story told uncommonly well."
— *Starred review, School Library Journal*

$9.95 • pb • 1-55039-142-9-X • Teen fiction ages 12+

★ Saskatchewan Young Readers' Snow Willow Award Nominee
★ The Stellar Award: the Teen Readers' Choice Award of B.C. Nominee

ABOUT THE AUTHOR

Heather, Yetsa and Sylvia.

SYLVIA OLSEN is a community development consultant who specializes in First Nations housing. She has lived in First Nations for the past thirty-three years. Her extensive experience as a researcher and front-line worker includes governance and treaty issues, many community research projects, and work at federal, provincial, and local levels to improve First Nations housing. However, it was Sylvia's personal experience as a mother of a teen mother and as a grandmother that motivated her to create a forum for teen mothers and to write *Just Ask Us*. Sylvia has written six novels for young people, including *The Girl with a Baby*, which is about Jane, a fourteen-year-old who has a baby. Sylvia lives on the Saanich Peninsula just north of Victoria, British Columbia.